Oxford AQA GCSE History (9-1)

Conflict and Tension in Asia 1950-1975

Revision Guide

 RECAP  APPLY  REVIEW ✓ SUCCEED

Lindsay Bruce
Aaron Wilkes

SERIES EDITOR
Aaron Wilkes

OXFORD

OXFORD
UNIVERSITY PRESS

Great Clarendon Street, Oxford, OX2 6DP, United Kingdom

Oxford University Press is a department of the University of Oxford.

It furthers the University's objective of excellence in research, scholarship, and education by publishing worldwide. Oxford is a registered trade mark of Oxford University Press in the UK and in certain other countries.

© Oxford University Press 2018

British Library Cataloguing in Publication Data

Data available

978-0-19-843286-9

Digital edition 978-0-19-843287-6

5 7 9 10 8 6

Paper used in the production of this book is a natural, recyclable product made from wood grown in sustainable forests.

The manufacturing process conforms to the environmental regulations of the country of origin.

Printed in Great Britain by Bell and Bain Ltd. Glasgow

Acknowledgements

Cover: Bettmann/Getty

Artworks: QBS Learning

Photos: p15: The New Zealand Herald/Newspix.co.uk; **p19:** Granger Historical Picture Archive/Alamy Stock Photo; **p21:** Everett Collection/Mary Evans; **p23:** Everett Collection Historical/Alamy Stock Photo; **p31:** Catholic Library Services/Library of Congress; **p33:** A 1964 Herblock Cartoon, © The Herb Block Foundation; **p35:** Mirrorpix; **p45:** Telegraph Media Group Ltd/British Cartoon Archive, University of Kent; **p47:** John Filo/Getty Images; **p49:** A 1968 Herblock cartoon © The Herb Block Foundation; **p53:** A 1972 Herblock Cartoon, © The Herb Block Foundation; **p55:** A 1970 Herblock Cartoon, © The Herb Block Foundation; **p57:** A 1965 Herblock Cartoon, © The Herb Block Foundation; **p58:** Library of Congress with permission from The Washington Post News Service and Syndicate Library; **p59:** The Advertising Archives;

The publisher would like to thank Jon Cloake for his work on the Student Book on which this Revision Guide is based and Ellen Longley for reviewing this Revision Guide.

We are grateful to the following for permission to include extracts from copyright material:

Walter Cronkite: CBS News broadcast from Vietnam, 27 February 1968, used by permission of CBS News.

Dwight D Eisenhower: *The President's News Conference*, 7 April 1954. Online by Gerhard Peters and John T Woolley, *The American Presidency Project*, http://www.presidency.ucsb.edu/ws/?pid=10202; used by permission of John Woolley.

Ian Hislop: Commentary on *Not Forgotten: Soldiers of Empire*, Channel 4, November 2009, used by permission of Casarotto Ramsay and Associates Ltd on behalf of Ian Hislop.

We have made every effort to trace and contact all copyright holders before publication. If notified of any errors or omissions, the publisher will be happy to rectify these at the earliest opportunity.

Contents

Introduction to this Revision Guide 5

Top revision tips 6

Master your exam skills 7

How to master source questions 8

How to master 'how useful are the sources' questions 8

How to master 'write an account' questions 9

How to master 'how far do you agree' questions 9

AQA GCSE History mark schemes. 10

Conflict and Tension in Asia 1950–1975 Timeline. 11

| | RECAP | APPLY | REVIEW |

Part one:

Conflict in Korea

1 The causes of the Korean War — 12

The Cold War 12

Korea and the Cold War, China, the USSR and the United Nations 14

The Korean War, Responses to the invasion 16

2 The development of the Korean War — 18

The United Nations at war, Advance into North Korea, China enters the war . . . 18

3 The end of the Korean War — 20

Stalemate 20

Peace talks and the armistice. 21

The impact of the Korean War 22

Part two:

Escalation of conflict in Vietnam

4 The end of French colonial rule — 24

The French in Asia, Dien Bien Phu. 24

The Geneva Agreement, 1954 25

Civil war in South Vietnam, Opposition to Diem 26

Civil war – the two sides, Who were the Vietcong? 28

5 The US involvement in Vietnam — 30

US involvement, The Domino Theory 30

Eisenhower and Kennedy. 32

Strategic Hamlet Programme 33

Contents

RECAP APPLY REVIEW

6 Johnson's war   **34**

President Johnson and the Gulf of Tonkin 34

Mass bombing campaign 35

Vietcong tactics 36

The US response to Vietcong tactics 38

The impact of US tactics 39

The Tet Offensive, My Lai... 40

Demands for peace and student protest 42

Part three:

The ending of conflict in Vietnam

7 Nixon's war   **44**

President Nixon and the widening of the war, The widening of the war:
    Cambodia and Laos 44

China and the USSR 45

8 Opposition to war   **46**

Growing opposition, Kent State University............................... 46

Importance of the media and TV, The impact of the Tet Offensive........... 48

The media and TV: influencing public opinion, The Watergate scandal....... 50

9 The end of the war   **52**

The US withdrawal from Vietnam, The Paris peace talks 52

The end of the Vietnam War 54

The Vietnam war: costs and consequences.............................. 56

Exam practice: Source analysis questions............................. 58

Exam practice: 'Write an account' questions 61

Exam practice: 'How far do you agree' questions 62

Activity answers guidance.. 64

Glossary.. 72

Introduction

The *Oxford AQA GCSE History* textbook series has been developed by an expert team led by Jon Cloake and Aaron Wilkes. This matching Revision Guide offers you step-by-step strategies to master your AQA Wider World Depth Study: Conflict and Tension exam skills, and the structured revision approach of **Recap, Apply and Review** to prepare you for exam success.

Use the Progress checklists on pages 3–4 to keep track of your revision, and use the traffic light feature on each page to monitor your confidence level on each topic. Other exam practice and revision features include Top revision tips on page 6, and the 'How to...' guides for each exam question type on pages 7–9.

 RECAP Each chapter recaps key events and developments through easy-to-digest chunks and visual diagrams. **Key terms** appear in bold and red; they are defined in the glossary. indicates the relevant Oxford AQA History Student Book pages so you could easily reread the textbook for further revision.

SUMMARY highlights the most important facts at the end of each chapter.

TIMELINE provides a short list of dates to help you remember key events.

 APPLY Each revision activity is designed to help drill your understanding of facts, and then progress towards applying your knowledge to exam questions.

These targeted revision activities are written specifically for this guide, which will help you apply your knowledge towards the four exam questions in your AQA Conflict and Tension exam paper:

SOURCE ANALYSIS   **HOW FAR DO YOU AGREE?**   **WRITE AN ACCOUNT**

 Examiner Tip highlights key parts of an exam question, and gives you hints on how to avoid common mistakes in exams.

 Revision Skills provides different revision techniques. Research shows that using a variety of revision styles can help cement your revision.

 Review gives you helpful reminders about how to check your answers and how to revise further.

 REVIEW Throughout each chapter, you can review and reflect on the work you have done, and find advice on how to further refresh your knowledge.

You can tick off the Review column from the progress checklist as you work through this Revision Guide. **Activity answers guidance** and the **Exam practice** sections with full sample student answers also help you to review your own work.

Top revision tips

Getting your revision right

It is perfectly natural to feel anxious when exam time approaches. The best way to keep on top of the stress is to be organised!

3 months to go

Plan: create a realistic revision timetable, and stick to it!

Track your progress: use the Progress checklists (pages 3–4) to help you track your revision. It will help you stick to your revision plan.

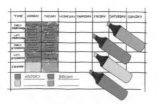

Be realistic: revise in regular, small chunks, of around 30 minutes. Reward yourself with 10 minute breaks – you will be amazed how much more you'll remember.

Positive thinking: motivate yourself by turning your negative thoughts to positive ones. Instead of asking *'why can't I remember this topic at all?'* ask yourself *'what different techniques can I try to improve my memory?'*

Organise: make sure you have everything you need – your revision books, coloured pens, index cards, sticky notes, paper, etc. Find a quiet place where you are comfortable. Divide your notes into sections that are easy to use.

Timeline: create a timeline with colour-coded sticky notes, to make sure you remember important dates relating to the three parts of the Conflict and Tension Wider World Depth Study (use the Timeline on page 11 as a starting point).

Practise: ask your teachers for practice questions or past papers.

Revision techniques

Using a variety of revision techniques can help you remember information, so try out different methods:

- Make **flashcards**, using both sides of the card to test yourself on key figures, dates, and definitions
- **Colour-code** your notebooks
- **Reread** your textbook or copy out your notes
- Create **mind-maps** for complicated topics
- Draw **pictures** and symbols that spring to mind
- Group study
- Find a **buddy** or group to revise with and test you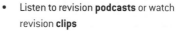
- Listen to revision **podcasts** or watch revision **clips**
- Work through the **revision activities** in this guide.

Revision tips to help you pass your Conflict and Tension exam

---

1 month to go

Key concepts: make sure you understand key concepts for this topic, such as nationalism, communism, tension, conflict, international co-operation, peace talks, guerilla tactics and public opinion. If you're unsure, attend your school revision sessions and ask your teacher to go through the concept again.

Identify your weaknesses: which topics or question types are easier and which are more challenging for you? Schedule more time to revise the challenging topics or question types.

Make it stick: find memorable ways to remember chronology, using fun rhymes, or doodles, for example.

Take a break: do something completely different during breaks – listen to music, take a short walk, make a cup of tea, for example.

Check your answers: answer the exam questions in this guide, then check the Activity answers guidance at the end of the guide to practise applying your knowledge to exam questions.

Understand your mark scheme: review the Mark scheme (page 10) for each exam question, and make sure you understand how you will be marked.

Master your exam skills: study and remember the How to master your exam skills steps (pages 7–9) for each AQA question type – it will help you plan your answers quickly!

Time yourself: practise making plans and answering exam questions within the recommended time limits.

Take mock exams seriously: you can learn from them how to manage your time better under exam conditions.

Rest well: make sure your phone and laptop are put away at least an hour before bed. This will help you rest better.

On the big day

Sleep early: don't work through the night; get a good night's sleep.

Be prepared: make sure you know where and when the exam is, and leave plenty of time to get there.

Check: make sure you have all your equipment in advance, including spare pens!

Drink and eat healthily: avoid too much caffeine or junk food. Water is best – if you are 5% dehydrated, then your concentration drops 20%.

Stay focused: don't listen to people who might try to wind you up about what might come up in the exam – they don't know any more than you.

Good luck!

Master your exam skills

Get to grips with your Paper 1: Conflict and Tension in Asia 1950–1975 Wider World Depth Study

The Paper 1 exam lasts 2 hours, and you must answer 10 questions covering 2 topics. The first 6 questions (worth 40 marks) will cover your Period Study (Germany, Russia, America 1840–1895 or America 1920–1973). The last 4 questions will cover Conflict and Tension. Here you will find details about what to expect with the last 4 questions relating to Conflict and Tension in Asia 1950–1975, and advice on how to master your exam skills.

▼ **SOURCE A**

▼ **SOURCE B**

▼ **SOURCE C**

1   Study **Source A. Source A** supports/opposes… How do you know? Explain your answer using **Source A** and your contextual knowledge.

    4 marks

2   Study **Sources B** and **C**. How useful are **Sources B** and **C** to a historian studying… ? Explain your answer using **Sources B** and **C** and your own knowledge.

    12 marks

3   Write an account of how…

    8 marks

4   '…'
    How far do you agree with this statement? Explain your answer.

    16 marks SPaG 4 marks

REVISION SKILLS

Read the Period Study Revision Guide for help on the first 6 questions of Paper 1.

EXAMINER TIP

Don't forget to read the provenance (caption) for any sources you are given. It will give you valuable information and help you place the source in its historical context. You will be able to analyse what the source is saying (Question 1) and assess its value (usefulness) to the historian (Question 2).

EXAMINER TIP

Don't forget that you get up to 4 marks for spelling, punctuation and grammar (SPaG) on this question too.

REVIEW ↻

Throughout this Revision Guide you will find activities that help you prepare for each type of question. They will help you recognise what a good answer looks like and how to develop your ideas to get a good level. Look out for the **REVISION SKILLS** ✓ tips too, to inspire you to find the revision strategies that work for you!

EXAMINER TIP ⌖

Don't forget you will also have to answer six questions relating to your Period Study in Paper 1. Ensure you leave enough time to complete both sections of Paper 1! You are advised to spend 50 minutes on your Period Study in the exam.

How to master source questions

Here are the steps to consider when answering the question that asks you how you know the opinion of a source.

Content

Look at the source carefully. You could label what you can see, or circle anything that you think is important. This might help you to break the source down and work out what it is about.

Provenance

Look at the date and other information in the source caption. The caption will give you a clue about what event(s)/issue/topic it is about. Think carefully about the events you have studied. Which one is the source about?

Context

Think back over your own knowledge. What features of the source content or provenance fit with what you know about the statement given in the question (such as 'Source D opposes or supports something')? What historical facts can you use to support your answer?

Comment

Make sure you use your own knowledge and information from the source to explain how the statement given in the question (such as 'Source D opposes or supports something') is shown.

 Spend about 5 minutes on this 4-mark question.

EXAMINER TIP

Try to describe at least one part of the source that either praises or criticises the event/person, then explain how this symbolises the statement in the question.

How to master 'how useful are the sources' questions

Remember that this question is similar to the source question in Paper 2, but this focuses on *two* sources.

Content

Look at and read both sources and underline or circle any detail that helps you to work out what they are about.

Provenance

Next, look at the provenance for each source; is there anything about the Time, Author, Purpose, Audience or Site (place it was created) (TAPAS!) that makes the source more or less useful?

Context

Now think back over your own knowledge. For each source, write about whether the content and caption fit with what you know. Does it give a fair reflection of the person, event or issue it describes?

Comment

You now need to make a judgement about how useful each source is. Try to use the sources together. What could a historian use them to find out about?

For each source, make sure you explain what is suggested by the content – and link this to your own knowledge to explain your ideas. You should also explain how the provenance makes the source useful (or not!).

 This question is worth 12 marks. Spend around 15 minutes on it.

EXAMINER TIP

Don't forget that every source is useful for something. Don't start telling the examiner what you can't use the sources for; no source will tell you everything, so just focus on what it *does* say.

How to master 'write an account' questions

Here are the steps to consider for answering the 'write an account' question. This question involves telling the key moments of an event in relation to the topic of the question. You need to describe, explain and analyse how one development led to another.

Select the key moments

What will you include in your story? Spend 1 minute to work out 3–4 key moments that are *relevant* to the question. Make sure you organise the moments in chronological order (starting with the earliest). You must include 1–2 specific historical facts for each key moment and plenty of specific historical detail.

Explain the connections

Write your answer based on the key moments you identified, and explain how the moments connect together to cause the event to develop. Make sure you link the story to the point of the question. A top level answer will also include an explanation of how the tension rises with each event.

 Spend around 10 minutes on this 8-mark question, but remember that this needs to include planning time.

EXAMINER TIP

Use phrases such as 'this led to…' and 'as a result of this…' to help you link back to the question and keep your ideas focused.

How to master 'how far do you agree' questions

Read the question carefully

What statement is the question asking you to consider? The statement is located within the quotation marks. Underline key words in the statement to help you focus your answer.

Plan your essay

You could plan your essay by listing other reasons that caused the event/issue:

Stated reason 1	Another reason 2	Another reason 3

Write in anything you could use as evidence for the different reasons, but remember that you only have about 2–3 minutes to plan and 15–17 minutes to write your paragraphs. For each reason, choose 2 historical facts you are most confident about and highlight these.

Context

Now that you have planned which reasons to discuss, start writing your answer, which needs to link to your knowledge as well. Aim for about 4–5 paragraphs: 1 or 2 that explain the reason named in the question and your own facts to back up the statement, 2 that explain 2 other reasons and facts to back them up, and a conclusion that explains your overall judgment.

Conclude

This question asks you 'how far…' you agree with the statement, so make sure you come to a clear conclusion.

Check your SPaG

Don't forget that you get up to 4 marks for your SPaG in this answer. It's a good idea to leave time to check your SPaG.

 This question is worth 16 marks. Spend around 20 minutes on it, but this needs to include time to plan and to check your SPaG.

EXAMINER TIP

Make sure you keep your ideas focused; use facts you know to support your ideas and use the wording from the question to make sure you explain how each reason led to the event.

EXAMINER TIP

If you want to achieve Level 4, you will have to reach an overall judgement. Is there one reason that you think is definitely more important than the others? Why?

AQA GCSE History mark schemes

Below are simplified versions of the AQA mark schemes, to help you understand the marking criteria for your **Paper 1: Conflict and Tension** exam.

Level	Source question 1
2	• Developed analysis of source based on content and/or provenance • Relevant facts and reasoning are shown 3–4 marks
1	• Simple analysis of source based on content and/or provenance • Some related facts are shown 1–2 marks

Level	Sources question 2
4	• Complex evaluation of the 2 sources • Argument about how useful the sources are is shown throughout the answer, supported by evidence from provenance and content, and relevant facts 10–12 marks
3	• Developed evaluation of the 2 sources • Argument is stated about how useful the sources are, supported by evidence from source content and/or provenance 7–9 marks
2	• Simple evaluation of 1 or 2 sources • Argument about how useful the source(s) are is shown, based on content and/or provenance 4–6 marks
1	• Basic analysis of 1 or 2 sources • Basic description of the source is shown 1–3 marks

Level	'Write an account' question
4	• A well-developed answer, clearly structured and explained • Explains different stages that led to the crisis • May explain how tension rises at each stage or how each stage linked/led to the next 7–8 marks
3	• A developed answer, well-structured and using a range of factual information to explain causes and/or consequences • Answer is supported by relevant facts/understanding 5–6 marks
2	• A simple, structured answer, using specific factual information to describe at least one cause or consequence 3–4 marks
1	• Identifies causes and/or consequences of the event 1–2 marks

Level	'How far do you agree' question
4	• Complex explanation of the reason named in the question and other reasons • Argument is shown throughout the structured answer, supported by a range of accurate, detailed and relevant facts 13–16 marks
3	• Developed explanation of the reason named in the question and other factors • Argument is shown throughout the structured answer, supported by a range of accurate and relevant facts 9–12 marks
2	• Simple explanation of one or more reasons • Argument is shown, supported by relevant facts 5–8 marks
1	• Basic explanation of one or more reasons • Some basic facts are shown 1–4 marks

You also achieve up to 4 marks for spelling, punctuation and grammar (SPaG) on the statement question:

Level	'How far do you agree' question SPaG marks
Excellent	• SPaG is accurate throughout the answer • Meaning is very clear • A *wide* range of key historical terms are used accurately 4 marks
Good	• SPaG shown with considerable accuracy • Meaning is generally clear • A range of key historical terms are used 2–3 marks
Satisfactory	• SPaG shown with some accuracy • SPaG allows historical understanding to be shown • Basic historical terms are used 1 mark

Conflict and Tension in Asia 1950–1975 Timeline

The colours represent different types of event as follows:

 Blue: military events   Red: political events

 Black: international events or foreign policy

1945 — **August** – Korea is divided into two countries

1947 — US President Truman vows to fight communism

1950 — **June** – Communist North Korea invades South Korea

1950 — **September** – General Douglas MacArthur leads the UN invasion into South Korea at Inchon

1950 — **October** – China joins the war on the side of North Korea

1952 — **November** – Dwight D. Eisenhower is elected US President and vows to end the war in Korea

1953 — **July** – North Korea and South Korea sign a ceasefire

1954 — **July** – Vietnam is split in two – communist North Vietnam and US-backed South Vietnam

1960 — **December** – The National Liberation Front (NLF) is formed in Hanoi (North Vietnam) – known as the Vietcong in South Vietnam

1962 — **December** – The number of US military advisers in South Vietnam increases from 700 to 12,000

1963 — **November** – South Vietnam's President Diem is killed

1963 — **December** – 16,000 US military advisers in South Vietnam

1964 — **August** – The Gulf of Tonkin incident

1965 — **March** – 'Operation Rolling Thunder' starts

1965 — **December** – 200,000 US troops are now in Vietnam

1968 — **January** – Tet Offensive

1968 — **March** – My Lai massacre

1968 — **December** – 540,000 US troops are now in Vietnam

1969 — **January** – Vietnam War peace talks begin in Paris

1969 — **March** – US President Nixon orders the secret bombing of Cambodia

1969 — **June** – US troop withdrawals start

1969 — **November** – 'Vietnamisation' begins; My Lai massacre is made public

1970 — **May** – Four student demonstrators are shot dead at Kent State University

1973 — **January** – The Paris Peace Accord is signed

1973 — **March** – Last US troops leave Vietnam

1975 — **April** – North Vietnamese army captures Saigon – Vietnam becomes a united communist nation

CHAPTER 1

The causes of the Korean War

RECAP

The Cold War

The Cold War is a term used to describe the period of openly hostile relations between the USA (and its allies) and the USSR (and its allies) from the end of the Second World War up until the early 1990s. Each 'side' had different political systems. The USSR followed a **communist** system, while the USA was a **capitalist** country with a democratically elected government.

Communists believe workers should seize power from rich factory owners and businessmen, as happened in Russia in 1917

The government should decide what is made and what it should cost

Communism

A strong government should control things on behalf of the people, making sure that all people are equal

All factories, shops and land should be owned by the government – not by individuals who are only concerned with making money

Capitalists believe that people should be free to own their own property and businesses, and make money for themselves

There are several political parties and people can vote for whichever one they like

Capitalism

Individuals and businesses compete against each other to produce more and make better products using the latest technology

Workers get jobs in factories, in shops, and on land that is owned by businesses or wealthy individuals

The origins of the Cold War

Towards the end of the Second World War, the USA, Britain and France (capitalist countries) disagreed with the USSR over what to do with the countries devastated by war

↓

Britain and the USA felt that European nations – including Germany – should be helped to recover quickly and so return to a time of peace when they cooperated and traded freely with each other

↓

The USA was willing to pay huge amounts of money – through the Marshall Plan – to help this recovery

↓

But Stalin (leader of the USSR) wanted to keep Germany weak because Germany had invaded the USSR during the war, and he wanted to keep Soviet troops inside the eastern European countries he had invaded during the war

The USSR claimed Finland, Lithuania, Estonia and Latvia, and gained land from Czechoslovakia and Romania

↓

The USSR now either controlled these places directly, or governments under Stalin's influence ruled them; **Soviet** territory had expanded nearly 500 kilometres westwards and gained control of over 20 million more people

↓

Soon, helped by Stalin, communists took over in Bulgaria, Hungary and Poland

↓

Even Germany was divided in two, with Soviet troops controlling the eastern part of Germany, while French, British and American troops controlled the western part

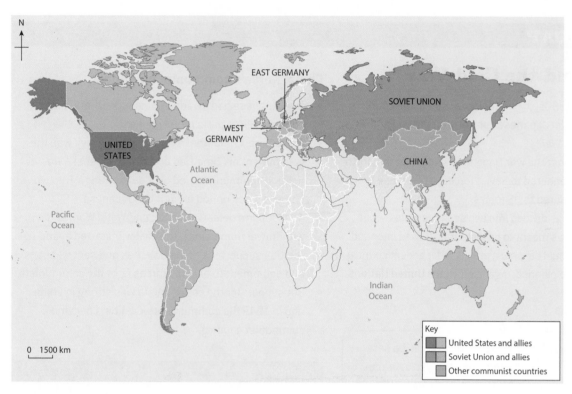

◀ *The areas of the world controlled or influenced by the two superpowers during the Cold War*

Key
- ■ United States and allies
- ■ Soviet Union and allies
- ■ Other communist countries

0 1500 km

The Truman Doctrine and containment

- In March 1947, US President Harry Truman said that the USA would come to the aid – with money and military help – of any country under threat of a communist takeover. The USA would 'contain' communism and stop it spreading from country to country.
- This policy of **containment** became known as the Truman Doctrine and was the basis of US foreign policy for years to come.
- Stalin was suspicious of the Truman Doctrine. He thought it was a way for the USA to control Europe by offering money in return for trade.

Tension increases

- By 1949, the USSR had developed nuclear weapons. Now, along with the USA, the two most powerful countries in the world each had nuclear weapons.

- In the same year, the USA, Britain, France, Belgium, Canada and other European countries formed a military alliance called **NATO**; this union was a defence against the USSR and its eastern European allies.
- The communist countries responded by forming the **Warsaw Pact**, a military alliance containing the USSR, Albania, Bulgaria, Czechoslovakia, East Germany, Hungary, Poland and Romania.

The Cold War is on

This was the beginning of the Cold War – a war of words, threats, bluffs and propaganda. It was a time when each 'side' feared the other, and a constant threat of nuclear war hung over the world. Each side spied on the other and built up their armed forces. Several real wars were fought, but not by US troops fighting Soviet troops. Instead, the USA, or its allies, fought Soviet allies – as was the case in both Korea and Vietnam.

⚙ APPLY

WRITE AN ACCOUNT

a Define the following using no more than 20 words for each:
- Cold War
- containment
- NATO
- Warsaw Pact.

b Create a diagram to explain the main differences between capitalism and communism. Your diagram can contain no more than 30 words.

c Make a list of reasons why the Cold War developed.

EXAMINER TIP

Your answers to these questions may provide some useful background information for any exam question where you need to explain the motivations behind actions or events.

Korea and the Cold War

- In the early 1900s, Japan took over Korea; the country remained under Japanese control until the end of the Second World War.
- When Japan lost the war, Japanese soldiers in the north of Korea surrendered to Soviet forces, while those in the south surrendered to US forces.
- The country was divided into two separate zones – but the division was meant to be temporary. It was intended that Korea should become a united, independent country.
- Elections were planned, organised by the **United Nations**.

A divided Korea

> In 1948, before UN-organised elections could be set up, the Soviets in the northern zone allowed a Korean communist named Kim Il-sung to take power.
> - Kim Il-sung was a committed communist and Korean **nationalist**; he wanted a united independent Korea. He had lived in the USSR from 1941 to 1945, serving as a Major in the Soviet army.
> - He had returned to Korea in 1945 to form the Communist Party of North Korea.
> - The north became the People's Republic of Korea (or North Korea) with Pyongyang as its capital.

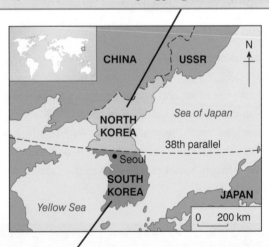

> In the US-controlled southern zone, elections were held; a capitalist with strong ties to the USA, named Syngman Rhee, became leader.
> - Like Kim Il-sung, Rhee too was a Korean nationalist.
> - He had trained as a lawyer in the USA.
> - He had developed a reputation for being a harsh ruler and his political opponents were quickly crushed.
> - The south became the Republic of Korea (or South Korea) with Seoul as its capital.

China: Korea's communist neighbour

- The Japanese had invaded China in 1931 and taken control of large parts of the country.
- At the time, China was in the middle of a civil war: the government of China (led by Chiang Kai-shek) was fighting communists (led by Mao Tse-tung). The two Chinese sides united to fight the Japanese.
- After Japan's defeat in the Second World War (and withdrawal from China), the civil war started again.
- The USA supported Chiang Kai-shek and sent weapons and equipment to help his forces fight the communists.
- But support for the communists was strong in China and in 1949 the communists won; China became a communist country.

REVIEW

America's support of Chiang Kai-shek's fight against communist forces is a good example of the US policy of containment in action. Remind yourself of this policy by looking at pages 12–13.

China's emergence as a communist country frightened many Americans who feared the spread of communism

US spies also reported that Stalin was attempting to help communists take control of other countries in the region, such as Indonesia, Burma and the Philippines

American fears

Senior US politicians warned President Truman that communists could soon be in control of the whole of Asia; the decision was made to stop any further spread of communism – by force if necessary

China, the USSR and the United Nations

- Within the United Nations, the big decisions relating to peace and security are taken by the 'Security Council'.
- When China became a communist country, the Security Council had to meet to agree to the new Chinese government being allowed to join.
- The USSR was keen for communist China to join – but the USA, unsurprisingly, **vetoed** the decision.
- The USA regarded Chiang Kai-shek and his supporters as the rightful government of China. In protest, the USSR stormed out of the meeting and refused to attend Security Council meetings for the foreseeable future.

The UN Security Council

- The Security Council has fifteen member states.
- Five of these are permanent (Britain, France, the USA, the USSR and China); ten are non-permanent and attend meetings on a rota basis.
- For a decision to be made, nine countries must agree, including all five permanent members.
- This means that any permanent member can veto a decision.
- At this time, the USA and the USSR regularly argued with each other in meetings and often blocked suggestions using their vetoes.

 **APPLY**

SOURCE ANALYSIS

▼ **SOURCE A** *From a speech by President Truman in March 1947:*

At the present moment in world history nearly every nation must choose between alternative ways of life. The choice is too often not a free one. One way of life is based upon the will of the majority, free elections and freedom of speech and religion. The second way of life is based upon the will of a minority. It relies upon terror and oppression, a controlled press and radio, fixed elections, and the suppression of personal freedoms. I believe that it must be the policy of the United States to support free peoples. I believe that we must assist free peoples to work out their own destinies in their own way.

▼ **SOURCE B** *A cartoon called 'The octopus of Chinese communism'. It appeared in a newspaper called the* New Zealand Herald *in November 1950*

a How did Korea come to be divided at the end of the Second World War?

b Why do you think the USA and the USSR focused on Korea at this point in the Cold War?

c Write a five-word sentence for each person listed below, explaining who they are:

- Syngman Rhee
- Kim Il-sung
- President Truman
- Chiang Kai-shek
- Mao Tse-tung.

d Read **Source A**. What are the 'alternative ways of life' that Truman is referring to?

e How does Truman describe the differences between the two political systems?

f **EXAM QUESTION** Study **Sources A** and **B**. How useful are **Sources A** and **B** to a historian studying US attitudes towards communism?

EXAMINER TIP

Try to find something different about American attitudes towards communism from each source.

The Korean War

The governments of both North Korea *and* South Korea claimed to be the rightful rulers of the whole of Korea. There were often border clashes between their troops

In early 1949, North Korean leader Kim Il-sung believed that South Koreans would welcome an invasion by North Korea. He visited Soviet leader Stalin to ask for his support

Stalin did not think the time was right – US soldiers were still based in South Korea and an invasion by North Korea might pull Soviet soldiers into a fight with US troops

The USSR began to supply tanks, artillery and aircraft to North Korea, and began to train their soldiers. South Korea had not developed its own army because they had relied too heavily on US troops

In the spring of 1950, Stalin believed the situation had changed because:
- US troops had left Korea
- communists had won the civil war in China
- the Soviets had developed their own nuclear weapons and felt more equal to the USA
- the Soviets had cracked secret US codes used to communicate with other governments around the world; they were convinced that the USA would not interfere in Korea

In April 1950, Stalin gave Kim Il-sung permission to invade South Korea – but made it clear that Soviet troops would not be directly involved. He said that if reinforcements were needed, they must come from China, not from the USSR

On 25 June, North Korean troops invaded South Korea

On 27 June, President Truman declared that the USA would go to the aid of South Korea. He also said that the UN Security Council must meet quickly to decide how to respond

Responses to the invasion

The UN response

- The Security Council met quickly.
- The USA suggested that the UN should assemble an army and help South Korea.
- The USSR could have vetoed this but were refusing to attend meetings at this time.
- The remaining members of the Security Council ordered North Korea to leave South Korea.
- North Korea ignored the request, so the UN agreed to put an invasion force together and take military action.

The UN invasion force

Sixteen UN member states sent troops to fight including the USA, France, Turkey, South Africa, the Philippines, Australia, Britain and Ethiopia

The USA provided the most: 50% of the armed forces, 86% of the naval forces, and 93% of the air force

General MacArthur from the USA was given the title 'Commander-in-Chief, United Nations Command'

> **REVIEW**
>
> Remind yourself why the USSR refused to attend Security Council meetings at this time by looking at pages 14–15.

The US response

- President Truman was facing elections in November 1950 and wanted to show the US public that he was trying to 'contain' communism.
- He ordered US 7th Fleet to patrol the seas around North Korea and South Korea, and sent troops and supplies to help South Korea.

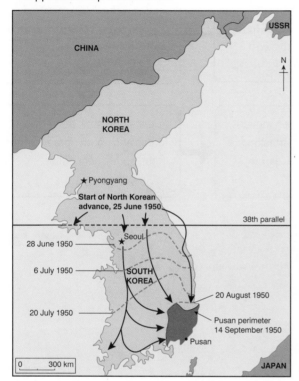

▲ The North Korean advance, June to September 1950; this was successful, pushing the South Koreans back to the area around Pusan

The Soviet response

- The USSR openly criticised the UN, saying that their charter (list of rules) stated that the UN was not permitted to get involved in 'internal events'.
- They said that the USA wanted to make Korea an 'American colony' which could be used as a US military base.
- The USSR confirmed they would not interfere with events in Korea.

REVISION SKILLS

Making revision cards is a good way of revising and creating a useful revision aid for later use. Jot down 3 or 4 things under a heading on each card. Try to include a factual detail with each point.

SUMMARY

- After the Second World War, a Cold War existed between the USA (and its allies) and the USSR (and its allies).
- The USA was determined to 'contain' the spread of communism.
- At the end of the Second World War, Korea was divided into two separate zones; the division was meant to be temporary and elections were planned.
- Before elections could take place, Soviets in the northern zone allowed a Korean communist (Kim Il-sung) to take power.
- In the south, the USA backed a Korean capitalist named Syngman Rhee: the country became divided.
- The governments of both North Korea *and* South Korea claimed to be the rightful rulers of the whole of Korea.
- In an attempt to unite Korea, communist forces from the north invaded the south in June 1950. The UN assembled an army to help South Korea.

APPLY

HOW FAR DO YOU AGREE?

a Create a timeline showing the key events in the build-up to the invasion of South Korea by North Korea.

b What role did each of the following play in the outbreak of war?

- Kim Il-sung
- Stalin
- Communist China
- President Truman
- The UN
- Syngman Rhee

c In no more than 10 words for each, summarise the responses of the following to the invasion of South Korea:

- The UN
- The USA
- The USSR.

d   **EXAM QUESTION** 'The actions of North Korean leader Kim Il-sung were the main reason the Korean War broke out.' How far do you agree with this statement? Explain your answer.

EXAMINER TIP

A question like this does not want you to simply focus on the actions of Kim Il-sung. You will have to think about other reasons why the war broke out before making your judgement.

CHAPTER 2

The development of the Korean War

The United Nations at war

The UN army in Korea was largely American, with the USA providing most of the military equipment. UN forces were led by an American – General MacArthur – and had to act quickly against the North Korean advance.

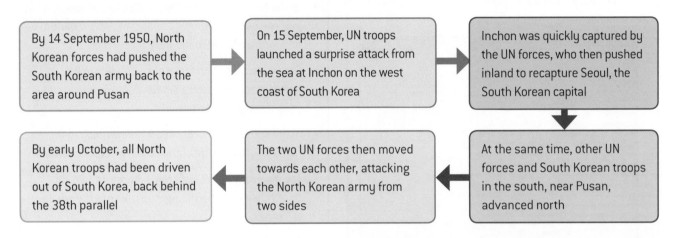

By 14 September 1950, North Korean forces had pushed the South Korean army back to the area around Pusan	On 15 September, UN troops launched a surprise attack from the sea at Inchon on the west coast of South Korea	Inchon was quickly captured by the UN forces, who then pushed inland to recapture Seoul, the South Korean capital
By early October, all North Korean troops had been driven out of South Korea, back behind the 38th parallel	The two UN forces then moved towards each other, attacking the North Korean army from two sides	At the same time, other UN forces and South Korean troops in the south, near Pusan, advanced north

Advance into North Korea

- In early October 1950, UN forces crossed the 38th parallel into North Korea. The UN approved this action, hoping that North and South Korea could be unified. The North Korean army was driven further northwards.

- China issued warnings that if UN forces continued to move north (towards China), China would join the war on North Korea's side.

- General MacArthur met with President Truman and confidently told him that China would not enter the war. He was wrong about this.

China enters the war

- When UN troops began driving North Korean forces back towards the Yalu River on the Chinese border, around 200,000 Chinese troops joined the North Koreans to fight back. The UN was now fighting China *and* North Korea.

- Chinese troops attacked with astounding force. They had the latest tanks and planes, supplied by the USSR, and an army committed to communism.

- Chinese and North Korean forces pushed the UN forces back into South Korea, and re-took Seoul.

- By March 1951, the advance had been stopped. Seoul was re-recaptured by UN forces once more. The two sides were roughly back where they had started – around the 38th parallel.

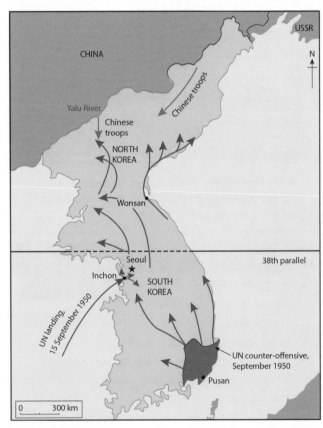

▲ UN troops attacked via Inchon in northwest South Korea and Pusan in the southeast

1 Truman felt that enough was enough, and defending South Korea was a satisfactory outcome.
2 He could still argue that communism had been 'contained'.
3 He was worried that continuing the war with China might bring the USSR into the conflict, resulting in nuclear war.

1 MacArthur thought differently. Despite being ordered not to, he sent UN troops back into North Korea.
2 He demanded a Chinese surrender, saying that the USA should be prepared to use nuclear weapons if necessary.

MacArthur is sacked

- Truman was furious with MacArthur and sacked him from his position as Commander-in-Chief of the UN troops.
- Truman ordered him back to the USA. The decision was met with uproar among the US public (because MacArthur was a well-known war hero), but Truman stood by his decision.

SUMMARY

- North Korean forces pushed the South Korean army back to Pusan.
- UN troops launched an attack at Inchon then pushed inland.
- UN forces and South Korean troops in the south advanced north.
- By early October, all North Korean troops had been driven out of South Korea. UN forces crossed into North Korea.
- China warned against the advance, but MacArthur was confident China would not enter the war.
- In late October 1950, China joined the war and helped push UN forces back into South Korea.
- By March 1951, the advance had been stopped, with both sides around the 38th parallel.
- Against orders from Truman, MacArthur sent UN troops back into North Korea. MacArthur was sacked.

APPLY

WRITE AN ACCOUNT

a Make a set of revision cards about the events of the Korean War up to this point. Jot down 3 or 4 things under the following headings on each card. Try to include factual details:

- The United Nations at war
- Advance into North Korea
- China enters the war
- Conflict between Truman and MacArthur.

b Why do you think UN forces crossed over into North Korea in early October 1950?

c **EXAM QUESTION** Write an account of how the Korean War became an international crisis in the early 1950s.

> **EXAMINER TIP**
>
> It is vital that you don't just write about the conflict, but explain how the conflict was a crisis in international relations.

SOURCE ANALYSIS

◀ **SOURCE A** *A cartoon called 'Not a General's Job', published in the USA in 1951, on the day before President Truman sacked General MacArthur. It says 'World War III in Asia'*

a Who was General MacArthur?

b Why was he sacked?

c **EXAM QUESTION** Source A is critical of General MacArthur. How do you know? Explain your answer using **Source A** and your contextual knowledge.

> **EXAMINER TIP**
>
> Remember to link your own knowledge to your answer. What do you know about MacArthur and these events that will help you understand the cartoonist's view?

 **RECAP**

Stalemate

After the advances and retreats made by UN troops and by Chinese and North Korean troops, by the middle of 1951 both sides were again facing each other from heavily fortified positions over the 38th parallel.

Air power

To try to break the **stalemate**, the USA decided to use their vast airpower. US planes began bombing North Korean towns, cities, transport systems, factories and military bases with high explosives and **napalm**. As many as one million people – both soldiers and civilians – were killed.

Soviet involvement

- Before China had become directly involved in the war, Chinese politicians had met with Stalin, the Soviet leader, to ask for his support.
- Stalin agreed to send military equipment and ammunition to help the Chinese and North Korean forces.
- He agreed to provide Soviet fighter planes (and pilots) but stipulated that they would be ordered to operate only over Chinese airspace, and around the Chinese–North Korean border.

A Soviet cover-up

REVIEW

Look at the map on page 18 to remind yourself where the 38th parallel is.

▼ **SOURCE A** *A telegram from Mao Tse-tung to Stalin, 15 November 1950*

Comrade Stalin,

I welcome your proposal to add 120 MiG-15 planes to the Belov Air Division, to send them to China to prepare to form an Air Force. With your help, we will carry out the strengthening of the anti-aircraft defenses at Andong Airport. In the past 12 days, thanks to the courage and efforts of the Soviet air force pilots in battle, 23 invading American planes have been shot down. Congratulations on this achievement.

Signed, Mao Zedong.

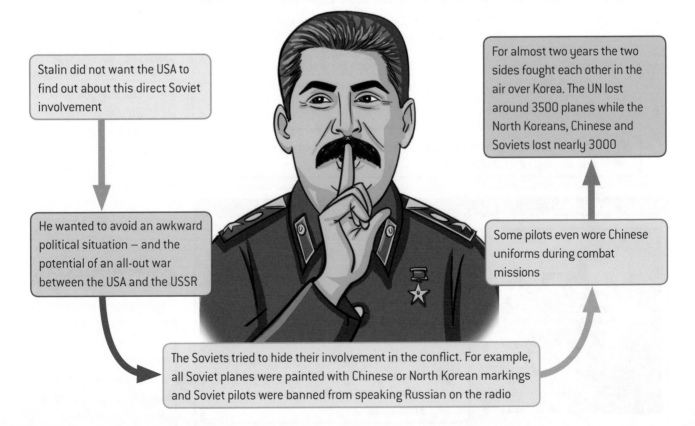

Stalin did not want the USA to find out about this direct Soviet involvement

He wanted to avoid an awkward political situation – and the potential of an all-out war between the USA and the USSR

For almost two years the two sides fought each other in the air over Korea. The UN lost around 3500 planes while the North Koreans, Chinese and Soviets lost nearly 3000

Some pilots even wore Chinese uniforms during combat missions

The Soviets tried to hide their involvement in the conflict. For example, all Soviet planes were painted with Chinese or North Korean markings and Soviet pilots were banned from speaking Russian on the radio

The MiG-15 Soviet fighter jets were much more technologically advanced than any of the UN fighter planes. Because of this, the Americans offered a large reward to any Chinese, North Korean or Soviet pilot who was prepared to defect – to fly to a UN airfield and hand his plane over to the Americans, who could then copy the Soviet technology.

► **SOURCE B** *A US air force leaflet offering a $100,000 reward for a Soviet MiG-15 fighter jet; these were dropped on North Korean MiG bases*

Peace talks and the armistice

Timeline

▼ **July 1951**

◼ Peace talks begin – but the two sides cannot come to any agreements

▼ **November 1952**

◼ President Truman is replaced by Dwight D. Eisenhower, who is keen for an end to the war

▼ **March 1953**

◼ Soviet leader Stalin dies. The North Koreans and the Chinese are not confident that any new Soviet leader will support them as Stalin had done

▼ **27 July 1953**

◼ The UN, China and North Korea sign a peace treaty that ends the fighting:

- Both North Korea and South Korea remain independent, separate countries
- The border between the two remains at the 38th parallel
- A three-kilometre wide demilitarised zone is placed between the two countries, to act as a buffer in the hope of preventing future wars

APPLY

SOURCE ANALYSIS

a Define the following terms in no more than 10 words each:
- stalemate
- defect
- demilitarised zone.

b List the ways in which the UN tried to break the military stalemate after 1951.

c Create a 10-point fact test to test detailed knowledge about the end of the Korean War. You can swap the test with a friend.

d

 Study **Sources A** and **B**. How useful are **Sources A** and **B** to a historian studying the war in the air in Korea?

 EXAMINER TIP

Make sure you mention how *both* sources can be of use.

The impact of the Korean War

No one knows exactly how many people died in the war, because some of the countries involved did not keep accurate figures – but the war was a bloody one.

The Korean War and the Cold War

- The Korean War was the first time during the Cold War that the new 'superpowers' had become directly involved in military conflict.
- The war meant that the Cold War had spread from Europe to Asia.
- The USA made additional alliances with countries in the east, such as the Philippines, Australia and New Zealand. It spent vast sums of money rebuilding Japan.
- In contrast, the USA cut off all dealings with communist China and instead gave their support to the politicians – now based on the island of Taiwan – who had controlled China before the communist takeover.
- The USA vowed to increase support (such as supplies and weapons) for any country fighting communism, such as the French who were fighting communist rebels in French-controlled Vietnam.

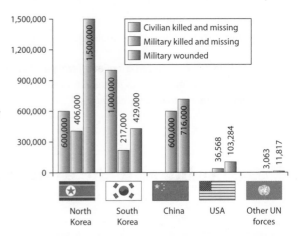

▲ *Estimated casualties in the Korean War*

Weapons build-up

Both the US and Soviet armies, navies and air forces increased in size at this time – the US army, for example, increased by 50%.

> The USA increased the number of army and air bases outside US territory in Europe, the Middle East, and elsewhere in Asia

> By 1952, the USA had around 750 nuclear bombs, up from about 100 in 1948

> The USSR also increased the quality and quantity of their nuclear weapons

> By the end of the war, the USA was spending 14.1% of its money each year on the war

> The 1950s saw the introduction of 'intercontinental ballistic missiles' (ICBMs): nuclear missiles capable of travelling huge distances around the globe, rather than having to be dropped by bomber planes

Gains and losses sustained as a result of the Korean War		
Gains	**Country/ organisation**	**Losses**
Limited: despite the ceasefire, Korea remained in a state of war, with no permanent peace treaty existing. However, relations between Korea and its allies became stronger. For example, the USSR cancelled North Korea's debt and sent economic aid in September 1953. China also cancelled North Korea's debt, gave monetary aid and sent experts to help rebuild the country	Korea (North and South)	• Huge civilian and military losses • 80% of Korea's industrial and government buildings were destroyed • Half of all housing and most of the transportation network was destroyed • North Korea suffered far greater damage
US policy of containment had stopped the spread of communism into South Korea	USA	• Large numbers of soldiers were killed or wounded • As well as the human cost, the USA spent billions on the war • Failed to 'save' North Korea from communism
• Role of UN was strengthened by the war. It was made clear that the UN would take decisive action and stand up to aggressive nations • USSR subsequently returned to various UN organisations	UN	• Failed in its aim to hold free elections and unite Korea • Some viewed the war as confirmation that the UN was hugely influenced by the USA. The commander of the UN forces had been American and took orders from the US President

Achieved a closer relationship with fellow communist state – China	USSR	The war heightened tensions with the USA, and forced the USSR into an expensive arms race with the USA
• Achieved a closer relationship with fellow communist state – the USSR • Was propelled onto the world stage as a major military power	China	• China was a poor country, and the war was very expensive • Failed to 'win' South Korea for communism • Trade and political links with the USA ended for almost 25 years

SUMMARY

- To try to break the stalemate in Korea, the USA used its vast air power and the Soviets sent military supplies to help the Chinese and North Korean forces.

- Peace talks began in July 1951, but they were initially unsuccessful.

- President Truman was replaced by Dwight D. Eisenhower in 1952, who was keen for an end to the war. Also, Soviet leader Stalin died in 1953 and the North Koreans and the Chinese were not confident that any new Soviet leader would support them.

- In July 1953, the UN, China and North Korea signed a peace treaty.

- The Korean War had a major impact on all the nations involved, as well as the UN and the Cold War itself.

 APPLY

HOW FAR DO YOU AGREE?

a List the ways in which the Korean War made an impact on relations between the superpowers.

b Create your own version of the gains/losses chart on this page. However, limit the number of words you use to 50. Use sketches, doodles, and pictures to help make facts memorable. You do not have to be a good artist to do this!

c EXAM QUESTION 'There were no winners in the Korean War.' How far do you agree with this statement? Explain your answer.

 EXAMINER TIP

You will need to provide a balanced argument here, writing about countries and organisations that gained and lost as a result of the war.

SOURCE ANALYSIS

▶ **SOURCE A** *A propaganda leaflet distributed by UN forces during the Korean War, 1950–53. It shows Korean people and a soldier being crushed by a skull-headed red python with a Russian hammer and sickle logo*

EXAM QUESTION Study **Source A**. **Source A** is critical of the USSR's involvement in Korea. How do you know? Explain your answer using **Source A** and your contextual knowledge.

 EXAMINER TIP

Make sure you read the provenance of the source carefully.

CHAPTER 4

The end of French colonial rule

 **RECAP**

The French in Asia

During the Korean War, the USA was also turning its attention to Vietnam, also in Asia. Although Vietnam was under French control, by 1950 there was a strong communist presence there. The USA wanted to contain this communism and stop it spreading.

France had taken control of many countries in Southeast Asia during the eighteenth century as a way to extend its **empire**. The area became known as French Indochina, and opened up a huge market into which France could import and sell its goods. France also made money from the valuable raw materials – rubber, tin, zinc and coal – found in the area. But during the 1940s French control started to weaken, leading to a period of conflict known as the First Indochina War.

The First Indochina War, 1946–54

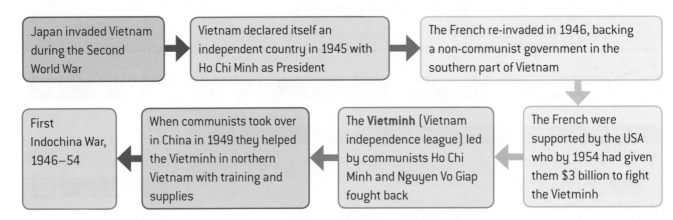

Japan invaded Vietnam during the Second World War → Vietnam declared itself an independent country in 1945 with Ho Chi Minh as President → The French re-invaded in 1946, backing a non-communist government in the southern part of Vietnam

First Indochina War, 1946–54 ← When communists took over in China in 1949 they helped the Vietminh in northern Vietnam with training and supplies ← The **Vietminh** (Vietnam independence league) led by communists Ho Chi Minh and Nguyen Vo Giap fought back ← The French were supported by the USA who by 1954 had given them $3 billion to fight the Vietminh

Dien Bien Phu

- French control of Hanoi in November 1946 pushed the Vietminh into the jungle, where they used guerrilla 'hit and run' tactics to harass the well-equipped French troops.
- The French retaliated by attacking peasant villages; this only increased support for the Vietminh.
- A key turning point in the war was the Battle of Dien Bien Phu.

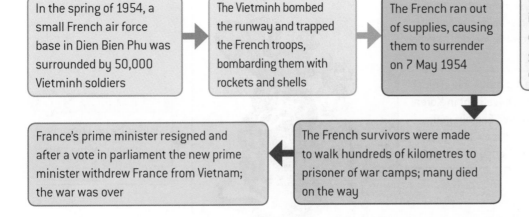

In the spring of 1954, a small French air force base in Dien Bien Phu was surrounded by 50,000 Vietminh soldiers → The Vietminh bombed the runway and trapped the French troops, bombarding them with rockets and shells → The French ran out of supplies, causing them to surrender on 7 May 1954

France's prime minister resigned and after a vote in parliament the new prime minister withdrew France from Vietnam; the war was over ← The French survivors were made to walk hundreds of kilometres to prisoner of war camps; many died on the way

> **REVISION SKILLS**
>
> There are lots of new people, places and groups in this chapter. Make a flashcard for each, with no more than three pieces of information about each one. This will stop you getting confused in the exam.

The Geneva Agreement, 1954

After the First Indochina War, leaders representing all sides of the Vietnam conflict, along with leaders from Britain, China, the USSR and the USA, met in Geneva, Switzerland in 1954. The aim of the conference was to find a peaceful solution. Western powers were keen to delay elections in Vietnam as they were worried about the high level of support for the communist leader Ho Chi Minh. They agreed to the following:

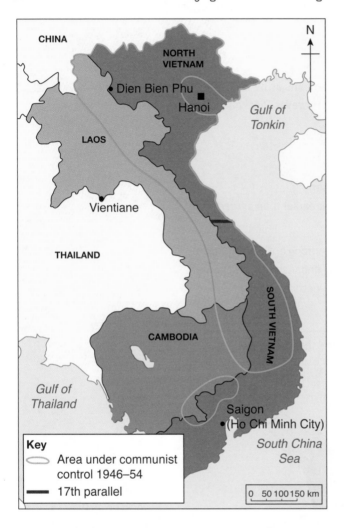

AGREED

- Vietnam would be divided at the 17th parallel
- Ho Chi Minh would rule North Vietnam
- Ngo Dinh Diem would rule South Vietnam
- The French would leave Vietnam
- The Vietminh would leave South Vietnam
- Vietnamese citizens could live in whichever part of Vietnam they chose
- A general election would be held before July 1956
- Laos and Cambodia would be independent countries

▲ A map of Indochina showing Vietnam split into North and South

 APPLY

WRITE AN ACCOUNT

a Using five cards, write down five key events in Vietnam up until 1954. Write one event on each card.

b Put the cards in chronological order on an A3 piece of paper and then draw lines between the cards with events that link them together. You should annotate the lines to explain the links.

c **EXAM QUESTION** Write an account of how the division of Vietnam into North Vietnam and South Vietnam was an international issue.

EXAMINER TIP

Use your cards from parts **a** and **b** to make sure the events you mention are in chronological order. You should think about how each event led to Vietnam being split in two.

Civil war in South Vietnam

The Geneva Agreement had been passed but not everyone was pleased with it. Both Ho Chi Minh and Ngo Dinh Diem wanted a united Vietnam – but they each wanted to be the person in charge. Both leaders knew the elections that had to take place by July 1956 would decide Vietnam's future.

Diem and South Vietnam

Ngo Dinh Diem was chosen as South Vietnam's leader by the Americans as he was anti-communist. The USA believed it could control and influence him. However, Diem had his own ideas of how Vietnam should be run. He created tension by:

- pushing peasants off their land
- giving key jobs to his family and friends
- punishing (sometimes by death) any people who opposed him
- calling an election in South Vietnam in October 1955 – a year earlier than agreed. This angered Ho Chi Minh and other leaders in North Vietnam.

But the Americans continued to support Diem because he was a strong anti-communist – and seen as the USA's best chance to stop South Vietnam falling under communist control. Running against Diem in the election was the former emperor of Vietnam, Bo Dai.

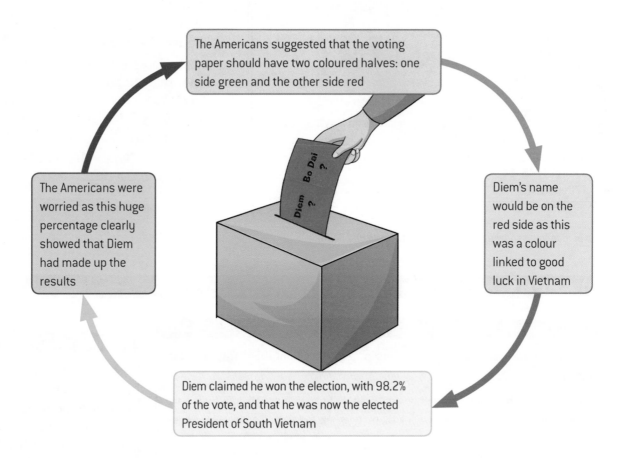

The Americans suggested that the voting paper should have two coloured halves: one side green and the other side red

Diem's name would be on the red side as this was a colour linked to good luck in Vietnam

Diem claimed he won the election, with 98.2% of the vote, and that he was now the elected President of South Vietnam

The Americans were worried as this huge percentage clearly showed that Diem had made up the results

Opposition to Diem

Diem's use of force and intimidation meant there were many groups who opposed him. Two examples were the **National Liberation Front** and Buddhists.

National Liberation Front (NLF)

Who: Political organisation in South Vietnam led by Ho Chi Minh. Initially the NLF wanted to get rid of Catholic power and influence in Vietnam, but it was quickly dominated by communists

Why: Nationalists who wanted land to be given back to peasants, and wanted to unite North and South Vietnam. The NLF wanted an administration that represented all social classes and religions

How: At first they targeted officials in Diem's government, murdering hundreds of them. Later they were encouraged by Ho Chi Minh to fight the **Army of the Republic of Vietnam** (ARVN) — the South Vietnamese army

Buddhists

Who: Members of the Buddhist religion that spread to Vietnam in the second century

Why: Most people in Vietnam were Buddhists who felt victimised by Diem, who was a Catholic. Diem introduced anti-Buddhist policies; for example, stating that Buddhists needed to have permission to worship

How: Buddhists went on hunger strikes and held mass rallies, and some set fire to themselves in an act known as **self-immolation**. This gained a lot of media coverage as the Buddhists would invite foreign press to cover events

REVISION SKILLS

Mnemonics are a great way to help you remember key events. Try to create one for opposition to Diem. An example is BEN (**B**uddhists, **e**lection, **N**LF).

⚙ APPLY

WRITE AN ACCOUNT

a Create a mind-map showing the reasons people opposed Diem.

b Explain why the following groups opposed Diem:

- NLF
- Buddhists.

c Why do you think Diem called an early election? Explain your answer.

d Why did the USA support Diem when he was not following the terms of the Geneva Agreement?

e **EXAM QUESTION** Write an account of why tension increased in South Vietnam.

 EXAMINER TIP ⊙

Start with Diem's actions in South Vietnam and how these led to opposition.

RECAP

Civil war – the two sides

Several armed resistance groups developed under Diem's rule in South Vietnam because of his disregard for the 1954 Geneva Agreement and his extreme actions against those who opposed him. This tension eventually led to a civil war breaking out in 1957.

The two sides in the civil war		
Those against Diem		**Those in support of Diem**
• Moved into the jungle to form resistance groups • Many joined the NLF, which had the support of Ho Chi Minh in North Vietnam • They smuggled military equipment from North Vietnam down the Ho Chi Minh Trail, which can be seen in the map	NORTH VIETNAM · LAOS · Ho Chi Minh Trail · SOUTH VIETNAM · Pleiku · CAMBODIA · Saigon · 0 50 100 150 km	• The South Vietnamese army (ARVN) had more money and weapons because they were supported by the USA • The USA gave the ARVN fighter jets and helicopters, and trained their soldiers • The USA launched a propaganda campaign, in North Vietnam, against communism

Who were the Vietcong?

In 1956, Ho Chi Minh sent one of his advisers to South Vietnam to assess the impact that various resistance groups were having in their fight against Diem's control. The adviser, Le Duan, told Ho Chi Minh that North Vietnam would need to send more support to help these groups resist Diem and pave the way for elections and a united Vietnam.

Ho Chi Minh encouraged the different resistance groups to join together to become more powerful. This led to the creation of the National Liberation Front (NLF), which then became known as the **Vietcong**. They were led by Hua Tho.

Vietcong: aims

- A government that represented all people in society
- Vietnam to be one, united country
- More rights and land for peasants to bring them out of poverty

Vietcong: support

- Both peasants and middle-class professionals supported the Vietcong's nationalist aim of uniting Vietnam
- Peasants wanted their land back so were prepared to feed and hide Vietcong soldiers
- In villages where there was less support for the Vietcong, soldiers initially used intimidation; however to ensure continued support from the peasants the Vietcong then introduced a code requiring them to treat peasants well

Vietcong: tactics

- The idea was to wear the enemy down using guerrilla tactics
- Attacked in small groups (cells) of no more than ten soldiers
- Targeted small army patrols or government positions that were not guarded well
- Did not wear a uniform, which meant they blended in with ordinary people
- Used the Ho Chi Minh trail to get supplies from North to South Vietnam

Diem was shot dead on 2 November 1963 after a **coup** by generals and soldiers of his own South Vietnamese army (the AVRN). The USA had withdrawn their support and protection from Diem when it became clear how much opposition there was to his actions and policies.

SUMMARY

- Vietnam and surrounding countries were part of France's empire, known as French Indochina, until the 1940s.
- The First Indochina War removed French control by 1954. That year, the Geneva Agreement was signed, aiming to bring a peaceful solution to the conflicts in Vietnam.
- Under the agreement, North Vietnam was ruled by Ho Chi Minh and South Vietnam by Ngo Dinh Diem until a general election would be held in July 1956.
- In October 1955, Diem held an early election, claiming victory.
- There was opposition to Diem's regime and civil war started in South Vietnam, increasing tension in the area.

REVISION SKILLS

Break down the information for a topic in different ways. For example, create a timeline with 5 or 6 key dates.

 ## APPLY

HOW FAR DO YOU AGREE?

a What were the aims of the Vietcong?

b How did America help the AVRN?

c Describe the military tactics of the Vietcong.

d **EXAM QUESTION** 'Diem calling an early election in 1955 was the main cause of the civil war in South Vietnam.' How far do you agree with this statement? Explain your answer.

EXAMINER TIP

The key words in the question are 'main cause'. It is, therefore, important to talk about the different causes of the civil war in South Vietnam. For example, you might discuss the early election, opposition to Diem, and North Vietnam.

REVIEW ↻

Go back and read pages 24–26 on US involvement in Vietnam and the Geneva Agreement of 1954. You could also use your answers to the activities on page 27 to help build your answer.

CHAPTER 5

The US involvement in Vietnam

 **RECAP**

US involvement

As part of a commitment to stop the spread of communism the USA had supported Diem in South Vietnam. This support initially involved sending military supplies and training ARVN soldiers. Eventually, however, US soldiers became directly involved in the fighting in Vietnam.

US involvement in Vietnam ultimately lasted from the early 1950s until 1975, under five different US Presidents. The fear of communism was the drive behind this involvement.

The Cold War

The Cold War developed after the Second World War because of the USA's fear of the spread of communism. After the war, communist governments (under the influence of the USSR) had taken over in many countries in eastern Europe.

US policy-makers believed that poor countries were more likely to become communist. Therefore, the USA gave money to poorer countries, to help them rebuild after the war and to reduce unemployment, which in turn would make them less likely to become communist. This US policy was known as the Marshall Plan.

> **REVIEW**
>
> Go back to pages 14–15 to remind yourself about the USA's involvement in Korea after the Second World War.

The Domino Theory

The **Domino Theory** is a phrase that sums up US fears about communism and the threat it posed in Indochina. It was coined by President Eisenhower in 1954 and described the belief that the USSR and China wanted to spread communism around the world.

There were concerns that then the countries next to Vietnam would become communist as well

Eisenhower was sure that Ho Chi Minh would win elections to unify Vietnam, leading to a communist state

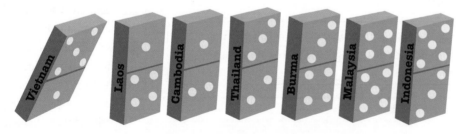

The Domino Theory led to a widespread fear of an eventual communist takeover in the USA. Many people were worried that Soviet spies were operating in the USA to overthrow the government. Those who were believed to be communist spies and sympathisers were investigated by the House Un-American Activities Committee (HUAC). The investigations by HUAC led to the following:

- widespread paranoia, know as the Red Scare, about the communist threat in America
- actors and filmmakers being questioned under suspicion of making communist propaganda
- the McCarran Act was passed: it stated that all communist organisations were to be registered and reduced job opportunities for communists

- McCarthyism: Senator Joseph McCarthy said he had a list of over 200 names of communists working for the US government. He accused anyone he thought could influence people but eventually took his allegations too far when he accused 45 army officers – with no evidence. People referred to his actions as a witch hunt.

This all made it easier for the USA to gain public support for their involvement in Vietnam.

▼ **SOURCE A** *From a statement made by the US State Department in 1956. The State Department is the part of the US government that advises the President and represents the country on international relations and foreign policy*

> The war in Vietnam is not a spontaneous and local rebellion against the established government. In Vietnam a communist government has set out to conquer a sovereign people in a neighbouring state. North Vietnam's commitment to seize control of the South is no less total than was the commitment of North Korea to take the South in 1950.

▼ **SOURCE B** *An American cartoon showing the Soviet Union overlooking the spread of communism*

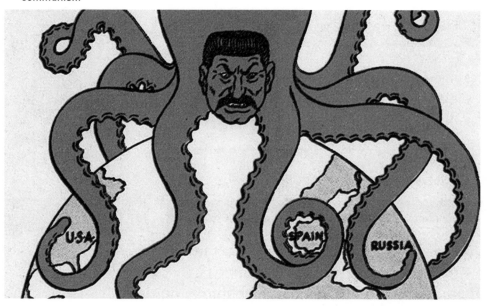

 **APPLY**

SOURCE ANALYSIS

a Write definitions of the following, aiming for around 15 words for each:

- Cold War
- Marshall Plan
- Domino Theory.

b Describe the Red Scare.

c

> EXAM QUESTION Study **Sources A** and **B**. How useful are **Sources A** and **B** to a historian studying American fears about the spread of communism?

EXAMINER TIP

Try to find something that the sources have in common about the specific topic of the question.

Eisenhower and Kennedy

In the early years of the USA's involvement in Vietnam, the government sent weapons, planes, helicopters and advisers to train the ARVN soldiers. The aim was to stop the spread of communism in the region while keeping American troops out of battle. Neither President Eisenhower (in office 1953–61) nor President Kennedy (in office 1961–63) wanted US troops fighting in Vietnam.

Dwight D. Eisenhower (1890–1969)

- Served in the US army and became a general in the Second World War
- Became President in 1953
- Ended fighting in Korea

REVIEW

Look back at pages 21–23 to remind yourself of Eisenhower's involvement in Korea.

John F. Kennedy (1917–63)

- Fought in the US navy in the Second World War
- Was the USA's youngest President and its first Catholic leader
- Took a strong anti-communist stance
- Was assassinated in 1963

Eisenhower's and Kennedy's involvement in Vietnam

Eisenhower's involvement	Kennedy's involvement
• Invited South Vietnam to join SEATO (Southeast Asia Treaty Organisation) to work with other countries to stop the spread of communism • Sent CIA agents to Saigon to gather information for the US government • Used propaganda to gain more support for Diem and turn the people of Vietnam against Ho Chi Minh • Gave supplies, money and military equipment to South Vietnam • Sent military advisers to train the ARVN • Tried to get Diem to carry out land reforms to keep the peasants happy • Did not force Diem to hold an election in South Vietnam in 1956	• Did not tell the US press about US involvement in Vietnam because he was worried about public opinion • Increased the money given to the ARVN. This meant ARVN troop numbers grew from 150,000 to 170,000 by the end of 1961 • Increased military experts in Vietnam • 300 helicopter pilots were sent to South Vietnam to transport ARVN pilots. They were not meant to fight but did have to defend themselves when shot at by Vietcong troops • Did not stop the coup against Diem • Supported the Strategic Hamlet Programme

Key:
- Political
- Military
- Financial

REVISION SKILLS

Using doodles and sketches could be a great way to help you remember the different kinds of aid each President provided. You could also sketch a strategic hamlet in your notes.

REVIEW

Go back and read page 25 to remind yourself why Diem not holding an election in South Vietnam in 1955 went against the Geneva Agreement.

Strategic Hamlet Programme

The Strategic Hamlet Programme was introduced by Diem in 1962 and supported by President Kennedy.

- It was described as a way to help South Vietnamese peasants defend themselves against the Vietcong.
- However, it was actually a way of cutting off the support the peasants had been giving the Vietcong.
- The peasants were moved away from their villages to 'strategic hamlets', often many kilometres away from their villages and fields. The 'hamlets' were surrounded by barbed wire and ditches.
- However, the programme backfired. By the summer of 1963 over two thirds of the population had been moved – and most were angry as a result. Many turned to the Vietcong.
- Kennedy had no option but to send more military advisers to support Diem and the ARVN.

▼ SOURCE A *A cartoon published in an American newspaper, the* Washington Post, *in December 1964. President Kenredy was assassinated in 1963*

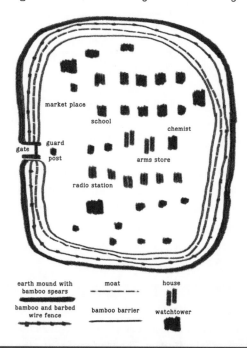

War Footing

SUMMARY

- After the Second World War the Cold War developed, leading to a fear of the spread of communism through the Domino Theory.

- President Eisenhower had been clear that US involvement should not mean combat troops on the ground in Vietnam. However, President Kennedy sent more support, including troops, to Vietnam.

- The Strategic Hamlet Programme was supported by Kennedy; this increased tension in Vietnam between US soldiers and many of the Vietnamese people.

⚙ APPLY

SOURCE ANALYSIS

a How did Eisenhower help Diem?

b What was the Strategic Hamlet Programme?

c What was the coup against Diem, and what happened as a result?

d **EXAM QUESTION** **Source A** is critical of President Kennedy's actions in Vietnam. How do you know? Explain your answer using **Source A** and your contextual knowledge.

REVIEW ↻

You may need to look back over Chapter 4 to remind yourself about the coup against Diem.

EXAMINER TIP ◎

First, work out what the source shows. Labelling a couple of key features might help you to do this. Then, link these features to what you know about the event. Do they link to a specific reason why Kennedy's actions in Vietnam could be criticised?

Johnson's war

 **RECAP**

President Johnson and the Gulf of Tonkin

In November 1963, Diem was overthrown in a military coup and replaced by army generals who had the support of the USA. In the same month, President Kennedy was assassinated during a trip to Dallas, Texas. He was replaced by President Johnson who had different views on American involvement in Vietnam.

Johnson's view on war

Lyndon Baines Johnson (LBJ) (1908–73)

- Was Kennedy's Vice President, so became President when Kennedy was assassinated
- Won his own election in 1964 and served until January 1969
- Wanted to create a '**Great Society**' that was fair to everyone
- Remembered by many for his role in Vietnam

Johnson had the following views on Vietnam when he took over the presidency:

- Like Eisenhower, he believed in the Domino Theory.
- He believed that if US support was taken away from Vietnam then communism would spread and would eventually end in a fight on US soil.
- He did not want to send more combat troops – this was particularly important as he wanted to be re-elected in 1964.

However, Johnson's advisers wanted him to become more involved in Vietnam:

- They knew the ARVN would not be strong enough to fight the Vietcong on their own.
- They believed that if North Vietnam was attacked then this would force Ho Chi Minh to withdraw his support from the Vietcong, making it easier for the ARVN to defeat them.

Johnson therefore approved Operation Plan 3A.

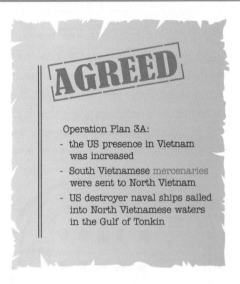

AGREED

Operation Plan 3A:
- the US presence in Vietnam was increased
- South Vietnamese mercenaries were sent to North Vietnam
- US destroyer naval ships sailed into North Vietnamese waters in the Gulf of Tonkin

The Gulf of Tonkin

The USS *Maddox* was one of the destroyer ships sent to support the attacks on North Vietnam. It did this by monitoring the signals sent out by the radar stations that were being targeted.

Timeline

▼ 3 August 1964

- Three North Vietnamese torpedo boats head towards the *Maddox*. The *Maddox* fires at the boats and they fire three missiles back
- US jets sink one of the boats and damage the other two

▼ 4 August 1964

- A report comes in from the *Maddox* saying that North Vietnam is going to launch another attack
- The US captain who raised the alarm then says he is not sure if the attack is taking place and that his men had not been reading the sonar properly
- Johnson launches an attack on North Vietnam anyway

▼ 7 August 1964

- The US government approves the Gulf of Tonkin Resolution. This gives Johnson the power to take any military measure necessary to defend South Vietnam and stop the spread of communism throughout Southeast Asia

Mass bombing campaign

Johnson made quick use of the Gulf of Tonkin Resolution. Despite the increased US presence, the Vietcong – supported by Ho Chi Minh – continued to attack US bases in the south.

In February 1965, the Vietcong attacked Camp Holloway – a US helicopter base – destroying ten US helicopters, killing eight servicemen and leaving over a hundred wounded. On 13 February 1965, the USA responded with Operation Rolling Thunder:

- This was a campaign of continuous bombing in North Vietnam targeting important government buildings.
- It aimed to reduce morale and weaken support for Ho Chi Minh.
- Only meant to last eight weeks, it instead lasted three years.
- The USA dropped nearly one million tonnes of bombs during this time.
- The number of US marines in Vietnam had increased to 200,000 by the end of 1965.

Within a year of becoming President, Johnson had not only increased the US presence in Vietnam but had also seen the start of combat involving US troops. The war in Vietnam had started.

REVISION SKILLS

Timelines are a good way of organising events and they allow you to see how events develop over time.

▼ **SOURCE A** *A cartoon created in 1966 showing President Johnson as the dove of peace flying over Vietnam*

APPLY

SOURCE ANALYSIS

a When Johnson took over as President, what were his views on US involvement in Vietnam?

b How did Johnson try to combat communism in Vietnam?

c Why was the Gulf of Tonkin incident important for US involvement in Vietnam?

d What was Operation Rolling Thunder?

e **EXAM QUESTION** Source A is critical of President Johnson's actions in Vietnam. How do you know? Explain your answer using **Source A** and your contextual knowledge.

EXAMINER TIP

You must put the source into context, so think about how Johnson responded to the Gulf of Tonkin incident. What campaign did he start? Can you link this to a feature in the cartoon?

Vietcong tactics

While the US army and the ARVN relied on equipment and the latest military technology, the Vietcong used guerrilla warfare and their knowledge of the jungle. The Vietcong could not compete with the advanced technology but they could work at destroying morale.

Guerrilla tactics

- Retreat when your enemy attacks
- Attack when your enemy retreats
- Raid enemy camps whenever you can
- Don't wear uniform – blend in
- Work in small groups

REVIEW

Read pages 28–29 to remind yourself how guerrilla tactics work.

How the Vietcong fought

REVIEW

Study the map on page 28 to see where the Ho Chi Minh Trail went.

Using the Ho Chi Minh Trail

- A vital supply route that ran through Laos and Cambodia from North Vietnam
- Ran through thick jungle so the enemy found it hard to find
- Porters would carry supplies on bicycles or on ponies
- If the enemy destroyed one part, a new track would open up – it was impossible to destroy completely
- By the end of the war a porter could travel from North Vietnam to Saigon in six weeks. It would have taken six months at the start of the war

'Hanging on the belts'

- The Vietcong travelled light and dressed like ordinary peasants, who supported them with food. They carried reliable AK-47 assault rifles
- They stayed close to the Americans and ambushed them, easily disappearing into the jungle afterwards
- As the Americans did not know where or how the Vietcong would attack, this was mentally draining for US troops
- This close action was called 'hanging on the belts' – it discouraged the US from bombing the Vietcong, in case US soldiers were hit in the process
- Approximately 51% of US casualties were caused by ambushes

Creating a tunnel system

- The Vietcong moved underground to make it even harder for the US soldiers to find them
- The tunnel system stretched for 300 kilometres under the jungle
- It was easier to ambush the enemy from the tunnels
- The tunnel system had hospitals, workshops, bedrooms and kitchens

REVISION SKILLS

Doodles and sketches are a good way of remembering content. Try drawing Vietcong tunnels and booby traps. This can help you picture Vietcong tactics in the exam.

Setting booby traps

- Punji traps were sharpened bamboo stakes hidden in shallow pits and covered with leaves
- Sometimes the spikes would be covered with human or animal excrement which would cause infections in wounds
- 'Bouncing Betty' mines exploded one metre from the ground to target the stomach and groin area
- Booby traps created difficult conditions for US soldiers

Violence and propaganda

- The Vietcong attacked government and public workers in South Vietnam (between 1966 and 1971, the Vietcong killed 27,000 civilians)
- Propaganda posters were distributed; many showed the Vietcong overpowering the enemy, or women and children supporting the Vietcong

 APPLY

WRITE AN ACCOUNT

a What was the Ho Chi Minh Trail?

b What does the tactic of 'hanging on the belts' of the American troops mean?

c Make a list of the advantages that the Vietcong had when ambushing American troops.

d What do you think the state of mind of the American troops would have been when facing the Vietcong?

e

> EXAM QUESTION — Write an account of how the Vietcong fought a psychological as well as a physical war against American troops.

EXAMINER TIP

Write one paragraph for psychological war and another paragraph for physical war. You should then try to show how Vietcong tactics could be classed as both.

The US response to Vietcong tactics

Having one of the most advanced armies in the world, the USA believed it would be able to defeat the Vietcong easily. However, the peasant farmers who made up the Vietcong knew the jungle well and used guerrilla tactics to take the US soldiers by surprise. The US army had to vary its tactics to get the better of the Vietcong.

How the US army fought

REVIEW

Read pages 34–35 to see how the Gulf of Tonkin incident led to Operation Rolling Thunder.

Search and destroy

- As it was hard to tell a villager and a Vietcong fighter apart, US soldiers searched villages in South Vietnam
- They burnt and destroyed whole villages if anyone there was suspected of being Vietcong
- These raids were known as 'zippo' raids because of the lighters used to start the fires
- They removed any Vietcong bases they discovered

Bombing

- Operation Rolling Thunder was a period of continuous bombing by B-52 bombers
- Over one million tonnes of bombs were dropped
- Some of the bombs were 'cluster bombs' (also called mother bombs or pineapple bombs) – these were designed to explode and release 600 smaller bombs

Chemical warfare

- The USA used chemical weapons – most famously Agent Orange and napalm – to destroy huge areas of forest
- Agent Orange was a toxic chemical that caused cancer and deformities in unborn children
- Napalm burned through jungle and forest but also through skin and bones

Conscripting troops

- The US troops were called GIs (short for 'government issue' or 'general issue')
- Their average age was 19
- They were conscripted for a one-year 'tour of duty' – refusal to join up could mean a prison sentence
- Their M-16 rifles jammed easily if they became wet or dirty
- Troops faced booby traps and mines in the jungle
- Many US troops mistakenly killed Vietnamese civilians because they were unable to tell them apart from the Vietcong

The impact of US tactics

- Supply routes along the Ho Chi Minh Trail were disrupted for a time but never long enough for the US army to get the upper hand.
- Few Vietcong were captured and most of the tunnel systems remained intact.
- The USA became very unpopular with the peasants of Vietnam.
- Support for the Vietcong increased as a direct result of US tactics.

 **APPLY**

HOW FAR DO YOU AGREE?

a List the problems the GIs faced in Vietnam.

b Give definitions of the following (use no more than 15 words for each):
- search and destroy
- Agent Orange
- napalm
- Operation Rolling Thunder.

c Explain why many villagers turned against the US forces.

d

> **EXAM QUESTION** 'American tactics were the main reason why the war in Vietnam went on for so long.' How far do you agree with this statement? Explain your answer.

 REVIEW

Go back and look at pages 36–37 to remind yourself of the tactics used by the Vietcong.

 EXAMINER TIP

Your answer to this question will help you explain why American tactics gained the Vietcong more support from the Vietnamese peasants.

 EXAMINER TIP

Explain the different mental attitudes the GI and Vietcong had about the conflict.

 REVISION SKILLS

Create a quiz about Vietcong and American tactics to test yourself. You can then share it with a partner.

The Tet Offensive

The Vietcong mainly used guerrilla tactics to ambush US troops and the ARVN. However, they sometimes launched large scale attacks in an attempt to defeat their opposition.

- On 30 January 1968, there was a temporary ceasefire in honour of Tet (a Vietnamese holiday).
- The Vietcong broke the ceasefire and attacked towns, cities, US military bases and the US embassy in Saigon.
- This attack became known as the Tet Offensive.

Tet Offensive: Why?

- The Vietcong wanted to inspire the people of South Vietnam to rise up against their government and US forces
- They hoped the US public would withdraw support for the war if they saw US forces being defeated

Tet Offensive: How?

- The Vietcong had been launching smaller attacks away from major cities to make sure there were fewer US troops in Saigon
- For months the Vietcong had been piling up weapons in homes around Saigon

Tet Offensive: US reaction

- US forces regained control of towns and cities quickly
- They used their advanced technology and training to defeat the Vietcong
- The US response seriously weakened the Vietcong by killing 10,000 fighters and 50,000 North Vietnamese

Tet Offensive: Impact on US military

- The US army had to use a lot of artillery and air power in its response
- By now the war was costing over $30 billion a year and over 300 US troops were being killed every week
- The US public began to doubt that the US army would win the war and if the human and financial cost was worth it

My Lai

After the Tet Offensive many US soldiers felt angry and frustrated: they wanted to beat the Vietcong. One such group was 'Charlie Company', part of Task Force Barker. Though they weren't involved in the Tet Offensive, they had suffered casualties during the month before the My Lai Massacre from Vietcong booby traps and mines, so they were keen to fight them.

Early March 1968: The US army had heard reports that a Vietcong base with around 200 fighters was located in the My Lai area, supported by the villagers; Task Force Barker was ordered to go on a search and destroy mission there

16 March, 7.30am: US troops landed and started firing at people in the fields and buildings they thought might contain fighters. Any villagers who tried to run away were shot or stabbed

Three armed Vietcong guerrillas were spotted and killed by gunships at the start of the operation, but no Vietcong were found by Charlie Company; there was no armed retaliation from the villagers who were mostly women, children and the elderly

When the US troops arrived back at base, they gave mixed reports about how many civilians and Vietcong guerrillas had been killed. Colonel Barker reported that 128 Vietcong had been killed while helicopter pilot Hugh Thompson reported seeing more than 100 civilians dead.

Charlie Company was praised for its actions

A year later, a young soldier wrote letters to politicians and military leaders telling them what had happened at My Lai. Two investigations concluded that Charlie Company had killed innocent civilians. The final reports also recommended action against the many men who had raped, murdered and participated at My Lai.

High-ranking officers were charged with covering up what happened, but the only person to go to prison was Lieutenant William Calley. He had personally killed innocent civilians. Many Americans believed he was following orders. He was sentenced to life in prison in March 1971 (but was released in 1974).

Impact of My Lai

- Many US citizens were left feeling shocked and confused about the aims of the war.
- People began to mistrust the people running the army.
- The anti-war movement grew and many people protested against the war – 500,000 protested in Washington in 1969.
- The investigations also exposed the low morale of the US troops in Vietnam.

Both the Tet Offensive and the My Lai massacre are considered turning points in the war.

REVISION SKILLS

Dates, facts and figures are important for supporting the explanation of your points. Always try to include some in your answers.

⚙ APPLY

WRITE AN ACCOUNT

a Who did Charlie Company think they would find in My Lai?

_____

_____

b What lies did Task Force Barker tell about its attack on My Lai?

_____

_____

c In what ways would knowledge of My Lai undermine American confidence in the US army?

_____

_____

d Identify five key words that you might need to use when answering the exam question below. Link each of these words to an event during the My Lai massacre.

_____

_____

_____

_____

_____

e

 EXAM QUESTION Write an account of how the events in My Lai in 1968 led to a change in US public opinion about the war.

 EXAMINER TIP

To help you develop this question further you could look at pages 50–51 about the role of the media.

EXAMINER TIP 🎯

Include an explanation of the feelings of many Americans about the Vietnam War before the truth about My Lai was revealed.

Demands for peace and student protest

Public support for American involvement in Vietnam had originally been high: many people believed it was important to stop the spread of communism. As the war progressed many people began to change their minds.

Changing public opinion

US tactics 	• Operation Rolling Thunder in 1965 led to an increase in anti-war feeling • People had supported the US helping South Vietnam stop the spread of communism; they didn't support the aggressive bombing of North Vietnam
The role of TV 	• TV reporters went to Vietnam – much of the fighting was filmed and shown on TV • The US public saw what was happening to innocent civilians who were victims of napalm, search and destroy, and Agent Orange • They also saw young US soldiers being injured and killed
The draft  FROM: DRAFT BOARD	• All men aged 18–26 had to register with the 'draft board' to ensure there were enough men to fight in times of war • Many men refused to fight in the Vietnam War – they were called 'draft dodgers' • Some moved to other countries to avoid the draft but others publically burned their draft cards as a form of protest
The cost of war 	• By 1967, the war was costing the US government $30 billion a year • By 1967, casualties had reached 15,000 killed and 110,000 wounded • Many young men returned to America after their tour of duty missing limbs, addicted to drugs, and suffering from the psychological impact of the war
Civil rights EQUALITY	• Martin Luther King spoke out against the war in 1967 • He was disappointed that President Johnson had spent so much money on the war and not on his **Great Society** priorities – education, housing, employment and healthcare • King and the boxer Muhammad Ali spoke out against the war because they felt the government should focus on racism at home and not fight people abroad

 REVIEW

Go back to pages 34–35 to read about why the Gulf of Tonkin incident led to Operation Rolling Thunder.

 REVISION SKILLS

Listen to some anti-Vietnam songs that were written in the 1960s, to help you revise. For example, 'Blacklash Blues' by Nina Simone, 'Vietnam' by Jimmy Cliff, and 'Fortunate Son' by Creedence Clearwater Revival.

Tet Offensive

Impact: Fuelled the anti-war movement and the change in public opinion as the events were seen on TV and in newspapers

Reason 1: Even after all the money spent on the war the Vietcong had easily attacked the US embassy in Saigon. The Vietcong did not look weak and this made people question the impact of the war

Reason 2: Many ancient monuments and cities were destroyed; huge numbers of civilians were killed; US soldiers were killed or injured. US citizens did not want to be associated with this destruction

Following the Tet Offensive and in the face of growing protests against the war, President Johnson refused to run for office in November 1968. He had faced much criticism from the anti-war movement and was replaced by Richard Nixon.

SUMMARY

- President Johnson agreed with the Domino Theory and was forced to increase US presence in Vietnam after the Gulf of Tonkin incident.

- The US involvement escalated dramatically when Johnson introduced Operation Rolling Thunder.

- The Tet Offensive and the My Lai massacre acted as turning points for public opinion, as it became clear that the USA was not winning the war and that many US troops were mistreating – and killing – Vietnamese civilians.

- The anti-Vietnam War movement developed across the USA.

 **APPLY**

HOW FAR DO YOU AGREE?

a Describe what happened during the Tet Offensive.

_____

_____

_____

b Explain how the Tet Offensive increased opposition to the war.

_____

_____

_____

 EXAMINER TIP

This is your first paragraph to the exam question below. Use the rest of the activities to build your full answer.

c Create a mind-map showing all the reasons for the increased opposition to the Vietnam War in the USA.

d Annotate your mind-map to show how the different reasons link together.

e On your mind-map, highlight the main cause of increased opposition to the Vietnam War.

f **EXAM QUESTION** 'The Tet Offensive was the main reason for increased opposition to the Vietnam War.' How far do you agree with this statement? Explain your answer.

 EXAMINER TIP

Use the wording from the question as often as you can to show that you are linking back to the question.

CHAPTER 7

Nixon's war

 RECAP

President Nixon and the widening of the war

After years of fighting, US forces had not defeated the Vietcong and had failed to stop North Vietnamese troops entering South Vietnam. President Johnson faced mounting opposition from both the public and government, and in 1968 announced that peace talks would take place to try to end the war. Furthermore, he would not stand for re-election.

A new US President was elected in November 1968. Richard Nixon was a **Republican** and had promised peace through a 'secret plan' to end the fighting.

Nixon's plan: Vietnamisation

- **Nixon's problems**
- He could not win the war using normal tactics
- It was too much of a risk to use nuclear weapons because North Vietnam was backed by China and the USSR
- If troops were withdrawn straight away communism would spread and people would question the main point of the war

Nixon had to find a way to reduce the number of troops in Vietnam – without losing the trust of the US public and without letting communism spread. He announced his plan – Vietnamisation – on 3 November 1969.

- Vast sums of money would be spent on the best planes, helicopters, tanks, machine guns and rifles to equip the ARVN against the Vietcong →
- The ARVN would be trained to a high standard to carry on fighting the Vietcong and North Vietnamese without the US forces →
- US soldiers could return home →
- By the end of the year 85,000 of the 540,000 troops in Vietnam had returned home to the USA

On 8 February 1971, ARVN troops attacked North Vietnamese troops in Laos

The attack was supported by US helicopters, bombers and artillery

The attack was a failure

Communists in Laos gained more support because of US/ARVN tactics

In March 1969, Nixon gave permission for the bombing of Cambodia

Nixon tried to keep the bombing a secret to avoid protest

In April 1970, Nixon ordered the invasion of Cambodia by US troops

The **Khmer Rouge** – a communist organisation in Cambodia – gained more support because of US tactics

Nixon called for 150,000 more US soldiers in Vietnam – this caused protests across the USA

Map labels: CHINA, NORTH VIETNAM, LAOS, Gulf of Tonkin, THAILAND, Ho Chi Minh Trail, SOUTH VIETNAM, CAMBODIA, Gulf of Thailand, South China Sea, N. Key: • one US bombing raid, 0 50 100 150 km

The widening of the war: Cambodia and Laos

Nixon knew that Vietnamisation would take time, as removing troops straight away would put South Vietnam at risk. The decision was made to destroy as many Vietcong bases as possible before the majority of troops left. Many of these bases were in neighbouring Cambodia. The Ho Chi Minh trail that supplied the Vietcong also ran through Cambodia, and Laos. Nixon gave permission for both of these countries to be targeted.

By early 1972, it was clear that Vietnamisation was not working. The North Vietnamese launched an attack on South Vietnam and in retaliation, in June 1972, the ARVN dropped a napalm bomb on an area of South Vietnam that North Vietnam had attacked. Innocent children were injured and killed – it seemed as if nothing had changed.

▼ **SOURCE A** *A British cartoon published in 1972. It is commenting on President Nixon's policy in Vietnam. The horse on the left is called 'No surrender' and the horse on the right is called 'Vietnamisation'*

China and the USSR

China and the USSR – both communist states – wanted to work with the USA to improve international relations. Nixon took this as an opportunity to push his agenda in Vietnam.

1970: The USA and USSR met to discuss the reduction of nuclear weapons. Nixon asked the Soviets to put pressure on North Vietnam to end the war.

February 1972: Nixon was the first US President to visit communist China; he asked China to persuade North Vietnam to end the war.

SUMMARY

- President Nixon was elected on the promise that he would end the war in Vietnam.

- Nixon introduced the policy of Vietnamisation.

- Vietnamisation was seen as a failure because of bombing campaigns in Laos and Cambodia.

APPLY

SOURCE ANALYSIS

a Write a definition of Vietnamisation – use no more than 20 words.

b How would bombing Cambodia and Laos help Vietnamisation?

c What did Vietnamisation achieve?

d In what ways were Nixon's policies in Vietnam failing?

e Describe what you can see in **Source A**.

f
> **EXAM QUESTION** **Source A** is critical of Vietnamisation. How do you know? Explain your answer using **Source A** and your contextual knowledge.

EXAMINER TIP

You must be clear about the ways in which Vietnamisation failed in order to back up the criticism in the source.

EXAMINER TIP

You can use sentence starters like these to help you answer part **e**:
I can tell that the source criticises Nixon's policy of Vietnamisation because …
This suggests that …
Vietnamisation was seen as a failure because …

REVISION SKILLS

Stick a map of the area on your wall to remember that it was Cambodia and Laos that neighboured Vietnam. Add notes to it as you revise.

CHAPTER 8

Opposition to war

 **RECAP**

Growing opposition

There were several reasons why opposition to the war grew.

The USA wasn't winning: the Vietcong and North Vietnamese army were still strong. Despite all the lives lost and the money spent, the USA was no closer to winning the war – this damaged people's confidence in their politicians and military leaders

Media coverage: images and stories of civilian casualties, poor discipline and drug-taking in the army were widely reported on TV and in newspapers

Casualties: there was shock at the number of dead and injured US soldiers. Around 300 died each week and the average age of a soldier killed in the conflict was just 23

US politicians: a huge amount of money was being spent on the war. Some politicians argued that the money should be spent on domestic issues such as education, housing and healthcare

Reasons for opposition to the war

The 'draft' system: nearly two million men joined the US army through the 'draft' between 1964 and 1972. There was intense hatred of this and many young people began to question whether the war was worth all the lives it was costing

The Civil Rights Movement: civil rights leaders spoke out against the war. They highlighted racial inequality in the army

Lack of support for the South Vietnamese government: many Americans felt that the government of South Vietnam was corrupt and brutal, and questioned why the USA was defending it

REVIEW ⟳

Remind yourself of the 'draft' system by looking back at page 42.

The anti-war movement

- Opposition to the war was particularly strong among college and university students.
- To them, the war symbolised the control and authority of government – and they wanted to rebel against this. 'Hippie culture' was popular at this time and its key themes were peace and love.
- In 1968 and 1969, there were many anti-war demonstrations – the largest anti-war protest in US history (500,000 people) took place in Washington on 15 November 1969.
- Sometimes the protests ended in violence, when police and students clashed.

REVISION SKILLS

Having someone test you on your notes and revision is an excellent way of checking how much you remember, understand, and still have to learn. Brief oral test sessions of about 10 minutes are best.

Kent State University

The most infamous student demonstration occurred at Kent State University in Ohio in May 1970.

Thursday 30 April 1970: President Nixon announced the US invasion of Cambodia →

Protests took place at colleges and universities across the USA →

Students at Kent State University arranged a protest for noon on Monday 4 May ↓

Weekend of 2/3 May: clashes took place between protesters and local police around the university and in the local town. The Mayor of Kent asked the Ohio state governor for help. Around 1000 Ohio National Guardsmen were sent to help stop further disturbances ←

Monday 4 May: around 3000 people gathered at the university – 1500 demonstrators and 1500 bystanders, who had gone to watch ←

Around noon: the demonstration turned violent – rocks thrown by students, tear gas fired by the National Guardsmen ↓

12.24pm: National Guardsmen shot between 61 and 67 bullets into the crowds. Four Kent State students were killed and nine more people were injured

▼  *A famous photograph from Kent State University; it shows Mary Ann Vecchio screaming as she kneels over the body of Jeffrey Miller*

Consequences of the shootings

- News of the shootings shocked the nation.
- Across the USA, many colleges and universities closed as two million students refused to attend classes.
- A similar incident occurred on 15 May at Jackson State College (an all-black college in Mississippi), when police opened fire during a demonstration, killing two students and injuring twelve.
- A government report concluded that the action of the guardsmen had been 'unnecessary, unwarranted, and inexcusable.'
- Eight of the guardsmen were arrested, but the charges were dismissed due to lack of evidence.

APPLY

WRITE AN ACCOUNT

a Create your own mnemonic or acronym to help you remember the different reasons for opposition to the Vietnam War.

b List at least three facts about student protests during the Vietnam War.

c Write an account of how student protests increased opposition in the USA to the Vietnam War.

EXAMINER TIP

To get the highest marks in these types of questions, you should structure your answer chronologically. Start with an account of the causes of the event, the event itself, and then write about the consequences or impact of the event.

Importance of the media and TV

Before 1960, there was little American coverage of events in South Vietnam. From 1960–64 about 40 American journalists covered events there but by 1965 this number had risen to over 400.

The rise of television

- During the Korean War, only 9% of American homes had a TV
- By 1961, this had shot up to 93% and television became the main way that Americans got the news

The influence of new technology

- New technology such as lightweight video cameras and voice recorders made news reporting a lot easier
- Unlike in the Korean War there was no government censorship. Independent reporters flown into the war zone by helicopter could report what they wished
- The full-colour horror of the war could quickly appear on news broadcasts in America

Early news reporting

- Media coverage was positive, focusing on the brave, skilful US troops
- The American GIs were the 'good guys' fighting communist Vietcong 'bad guys'

Media control

US ARMY NEWS

- Every day, the US army met with the increasing number of journalists in Vietnam
- These 'press briefings' formed the basis of the journalist's news stories
- As the war progressed, journalists joked that the army officials were not telling the true story of the war and were covering up how badly things were going at times

REVISION SKILLS

Draw – use sketches, doodles and pictures to help make facts memorable. You do not have to be a good artist to do this!

The impact of the Tet Offensive

The Tet Offensive, which began in late January 1968, was a turning point in both the way the war was reported, and the way in which the US public viewed the war. Until then, the US government had insisted that the war was going well. Now TV crews recorded and reported on the fighting in detail. The nightly news bulletins:

REVIEW

Remind yourself of the details of the Tet Offensive by looking back at page 40.

- shocked Americans who had no idea how brutal the fighting was
- caused people to question how much they could trust their government – what they were being shown didn't match up with what they were being told
- showed that the Vietcong could attack with great force
- made some Americans question whether they should be involved in this war at all.

Walter Cronkite

- America's best-known newsreader at this time was Walter Cronkite
- He was called 'the most trusted man in America'
- In a February 1968 news broadcast he said he was certain that, 'the bloody experience of Vietnam is to end in a stalemate ... it is increasingly clear to this reporter that the only rational way out then will be to negotiate ...'
- When President Johnson saw the report, he said, 'If I've lost Cronkite, I've lost the country'

 APPLY

SOURCE ANALYSIS

▼ **SOURCE A** *Adapted from the CBS news broadcast on 27 February 1968 by Walter Cronkite:*

> Who won and who lost in the great Tet Offensive against the cities? I'm not sure. The Vietcong did not win by a knockout but neither did we. The only realistic, if unsatisfactory conclusion, is that we are bogged down in stalemate and the only way out is to negotiate.

a How did the media cover Vietnam in the early 1960s?

b What was the impact of new technology on reporting the war?

c How were the media controlled?

d

> Study **Sources A** and **B**. How useful are **Sources A** and **B** to a historian studying the importance of the media in the Vietnam conflict?

EXAMINER TIP

Try to think what the cartoonist of Source B wanted the audience to think after looking at the cartoon.

▼ **SOURCE B** *A cartoon published in the* Washington Post, *28 January 1968. The cartoonist warns about American involvement in Vietnam by showing Uncle Sam holding an M16 rifle*

The media and TV: influencing public opinion

After the Tet Offensive and Walter Cronkite's news statement, coverage of the USA's role in the war became more negative.

Stories of US defeats – and more news films showing civilian and military casualties

- At the Battle of Hamburger Hill (May 1969), for example, around 70 US soldiers were killed and 400 were wounded taking control of the hill
- Soon after the battle the US quietly abandoned it, leading many people to question the whole point of the battle

New York Times

- In June 1971, the newspaper published leaked secret reports
- These confirmed the suspicions of many Americans that the government had been lying about US involvement in the war

Negative news stories

Stories about the poor morale and behaviour of the troops

- The coverage of the My Lai massacre in March 1968, for example, damaged the image of US troops
- An investigation revealed that they had massacred up to 500 South Vietnamese civilians
- The army's attempted cover-up led many more to distrust what the authorities were telling them

Life magazine

- The magazine shocked Americans by publishing the names and faces of all 242 US troops killed during one week of fighting in June 1969
- The sight of so many fresh-faced young men, now dead, brought the impact of the war right home

The Watergate scandal

Another factor that fuelled distrust of the US government was the Watergate scandal.

- President Nixon (a Republican) was linked to a burglary at the offices of his rival party, the **Democrats**.
- Historians are not sure whether Nixon knew about the burglary before it happened – but he took steps to cover it up afterwards.
- When his role in the scandal came to light, Nixon resigned.
- The scandal led many to question the country's leadership and think more critically about the presidency.
- It came at a time when many Americans were already unhappy with the government over its role in cover-ups relating to the Vietnam War.

SUMMARY

- The anti-war movement grew stronger, the longer the war went on.
- Opposition to the war was particularly strong among college and university students.
- The student protest shootings at Kent State University shocked the nation.
- Media coverage of the war grew rapidly during the conflict.
- After the Tet Offensive and Walter Cronkite's statement, media coverage of America's role in the war became more negative.
- The Watergate Scandal and the cover-up of the My Lai massacre fuelled distrust of the US government.

 APPLY

WRITE AN ACCOUNT

a Create a series of revision flashcards that help you remember the key facts about the influence of media and TV on public opinion. Use the following headings to help you:

- Tet Offensive
- Walter Cronkite
- Hamburger Hill
- My Lai Massacre
- *Life* magazine and the *New York Times.*

b What was the Watergate scandal?

_____

_____

c Why do you think the scandal had such a negative effect on the US government?

_____

_____

d  Write an account of how media and TV coverage made an impact on public opinion during the Vietnam War.

_____
_____
_____
_____
_____
_____
_____
_____
_____
_____
_____
_____
_____
_____

REVISION SKILLS

Be realistic when making flashcards. Don't include too much information by copying out all the information you find. Short bullet points, images, mnemonics/acronyms can all help you to remember things when you use your flashcards to self-test.

EXAMINER TIP

'Write an account' questions require you to do two things – firstly to write about something in particular (in this case, the media and TV coverage during the war), and secondly to write about the impact or consequences of an event, development or similar. So, with this question, you need to not only describe media and TV coverage during the war, but also address the impact it had on public opinion.

 **RECAP**

The US withdrawal from Vietnam

Richard Nixon became US President in 1969. He had promised the American people an 'honourable peace', and used a range of strategies to end the USA's involvement in the war.

REVIEW

Remind yourself of Nixon's policy of Vietnamisation by looking back at pages 44–45.

Vietnamisation: he built up the army of South Vietnam and gradually reduced the number of US soldiers fighting there

Pressure: he pressurised South Vietnam's leaders to work on a deal with North Vietnam. He asked China and the USSR to pressurise North Vietnam into making a deal

Nixon's strategies

Negotiation: Nixon's National Security Adviser, Henry Kissinger, negotiated with North Vietnam, hoping to bring about a ceasefire

Bombing: he increased the bombing of North Vietnam and supply routes in Laos and Cambodia; he hoped to force the communists to look for peace

The Paris peace talks

A series of public and secret meetings took place over a period of four years. Kissinger led the US delegation; he was convinced that common sense and practicality were the most important factors when dealing with foreign countries.

Timeline

▼ **January 1969**
- Peace talks begin

▼ **March 1969**
- US bombing raids on Ho Chi Minh trail in Cambodia begin

▼ **June 1969**
- First 25,000 US troops are withdrawn from Vietnam; 60,000 more by the end of the year

▼ **August 1969**
- Talks between the USA and North Vietnam begin – kept secret in the hope that discussions will be more open and honest. Little progress is made

▼ **December 1969**
- Final public peace talks take place

▼ **February 1970**
- Secret talks resume

▼ **April 1970**
- US troops invade Cambodia. Nixon announces that 150,000 more US soldiers are needed. A wave of demonstrations sweeps the USA

▼ **February 1971**
- US troops attack North Vietnamese troops in Laos

▼ **January 1972**
- Nixon announces that secret peace talks have been taking place. He says he aims to achieve 'peace with honour'

▼ **February 1972**
- Nixon visits China to improve US–Chinese relations

▼ March 1972

- North Vietnam attacks South Vietnam. The USA bombs the Hanoi and Haiphong areas of North Vietnam in retaliation

▼ May 1972

- Nixon visits the USSR to improve US–Soviet relations

▼ October 1972

- North Vietnam proposes an 'in place' ceasefire – they will stop fighting if their troops can remain in any territory in South Vietnam that they occupy. It is agreed that South Vietnam and North Vietnam will also hold free elections. Nixon agrees to support the ceasefire and promises $1 billion worth of military aid to South Vietnam

▼ 27 January 1973

- The Paris Peace Accord is agreed and signed

▼ March 1973

- The last of the US forces leave Vietnam

▼ August 1974

- Nixon resigns (because of the Watergate scandal). The financial support promised to South Vietnam by the USA does not happen

▼ December 1974

- North Vietnamese forces attack towns in South Vietnam. Over the next year, many cities, military bases and provinces in South Vietnam are attacked and occupied

▼ April 1975

- The capital city of South Vietnam, Saigon, falls to the communists. It is re-named Ho Chi Minh City. Vietnam is again a unified country, under communist control

REVISION SKILLS ☑

Make sure you know the question types you will be asked in each part of the examination. Find out how many marks there are for each type of question.

⚙ APPLY

SOURCE ANALYSIS

▼ **SOURCE A** *An American cartoon from the Washington Post, August 1972, when Nixon was running for re-election as US President. He first ran for election in 1968, and the cartoon shows him still holding the secret plans for ending the Vietnam War he said he had at that time. The cartoon is called, 'Now, as I was saying four years ago–'*

"Now, As I Was Saying Four Years Ago — "

20,000 AMERICAN DEAD SINCE 1968

SECRET ELECTION-YEAR "PLANS TO END THE WAR"

©1972 HERBLOCK

a For each of the following tactics, explain how it aimed to reduced US involvement in the war:
- Vietnamisation
- Pressure
- Negotiation
- Bombing.

b Create your own timeline of the end of the Vietnam conflict from January 1969 to April 1975 by selecting only 7 or 8 key dates and events. Use sketches, doodles, and pictures to help make facts memorable (you do not have to be a good artist to do this!). Try to limit the number of words you use.

c **EXAM QUESTION** **Source A** is critical of Nixon's approach to ending the conflict in Vietnam. How do you know? Explain your answer using **Source A** and your contextual knowledge.

EXAMINER TIP 🎯

Who is Nixon speaking to?

The end of the Vietnam War

In April 1975, the capital city of South Vietnam, Saigon, was taken over by the communist forces of North Vietnam. After 30 years of struggle in Vietnam, the conflict was finally over. The USA had failed to contain the spread of communism into South Vietnam, and Vietnam was now a unified communist country.

There are many reasons – or factors – that explain why the US approach in Vietnam failed, and why the approach of the Vietcong and North Vietnamese army was a success.

Despite having the very latest high-tech military technology, the USA often killed innocent civilians or even their own troops. This had a demoralising effect on the soldiers, and was a major impact on the anti-war movement back in the USA

A US soldier's 'tour of duty' was only one year long. After this time, they returned home. This meant soldiers never gained the necessary experience to fight in such tough conditions. Around 900 soldiers died on their first day in Vietnam

The guerrilla tactics of the Vietcong were well suited to jungle warfare

The Vietcong were far more experienced than many of the soldiers they were fighting. They knew their territory well and had been fighting long before US troops arrived in Vietnam. They had fought the Japanese during the Second World War

Many Americans questioned why the USA was fighting to defend the government of South Vietnam. They viewed it as brutal and corrupt

The Americans were fighting a long-distance war. Vietnam is over 12,000 kilometres from the USA and there were often supply issues with equipment and weaponry

Many South Vietnamese peasants supported the Vietcong. The peasants often helped the Vietcong

The discipline and morale of US troops was poor. Drug taking and desertion were common

The Vietcong were fighting on 'home soil' and were supplied locally or with equipment from allies in nearby China and the USSR

The Vietcong saw themselves as defending their own country against American invasion. As a result, they fought with brutal determination to defend their homeland. The Vietcong were motivated by the thought of driving the USA out of Vietnam and uniting their country

The media coverage horrified the US public. As the war went on, it became more and more unpopular. The anti-war movement was large and by the end of 1971 most Americans wanted the war to end as quickly as possible

 APPLY

HOW FAR DO YOU AGREE?

a Create a mind-map showing all the reasons why the USA was unsuccessful in the conflict. Challenge yourself by using only 50 words in your diagram – perhaps use icons and images to help you, rather than words.

b Shade or colour code the reasons – split them into those relating to the USA (this might be about their approach or strategy, for example), and those relating to the success of the Vietcong and the North Vietnamese army.

c **EXAM QUESTION** 'TV and media coverage was the main reason why the USA failed to win the war in Vietnam.' How far do you agree with this statement? Explain your answer.

SOURCE ANALYSIS

▼ **SOURCE A** *Adapted from a speech by the BBC news reporter Robin Day, speaking at a seminar to the British army in 1970:*

The full brutality of the combat will be there in close up and in colour and blood looks very red on the colour television screen … if there are one people in the world who are never going to understand the war in Vietnam it is the Americans who watched it on television. The war was meaningless to them: they don't know what happened at any single stage of that war and they never will and they are a lost generation as far as that is concerned and this is what worried me about television. The war was lost on the television screen of the United States.

"You See, The Reason We're In Indochina Is To Protect Us Boys In Indochina"

◀ **SOURCE B** *A cartoon published in the* Washington Post, *5 May 1970, called 'You see, the reason we're in Indochina is to protect us boys in Indochina'*

EXAM QUESTION How useful are **Sources A** and **B** to a historian studying American attitudes to the Vietnam War in the early 1970s? Explain your answer using **Sources A** and **B** and your contextual knowledge.

The Vietnam war: costs and consequences

The Vietnam War had a major impact on both the USA and Vietnam.

The financial cost of the war
- The USA reportedly spent just over $170 billion on the war (close to $1000 billion – or $1 trillion – in today's terms)
- It is estimated that a similar amount has been paid in benefits and pensions to Vietnam veterans who were injured, or to family members of dead soldiers
- Vietnam did not spend anything like the amount spent by the USA, but the country was made poorer and many people faced starvation during and after the war

The impact of the financial cost
- In the USA, President Johnson had promised a series of social reforms known as the 'Great Society'
- However, Johnson had to divert money away from his social reforms towards fighting the war in Vietnam

The environmental cost to Vietnam
- Between 1964 and 1973, over 7 million tonnes of bombs were dropped on Vietnam; they destroyed bridges, roads and irrigation systems
- Chemicals such as Agent Orange destroyed farmland and still cause cancer and illness among soldiers and Vietnamese children

- Most estimates put the number of Vietnamese soldiers (both sides combined) killed at around one million, with around two million wounded
- An estimated two million Vietnamese civilians were killed and another five million were injured
- About eleven million people became refugees during the war because their homes were destroyed by fighting and bombing raids
- About 100,000 children are thought to have been born as a result of relationships between local Vietnamese women and US soldiers during the war. Around 3000 were adopted by families around the world, but thousands remained, many of whom have led very difficult lives

- Around 58,000 Americans (average age: 23) were killed during the war
- Over 300,000 were wounded
- When arriving home to the USA, many troops faced negative reactions from both opponents of the war (who viewed them as killers of innocent civilians) and its supporters (who saw them as having lost)
- Many soldiers were affected psychologically as a result of drug dependency or because of the horrors they had witnessed

Human costs

- Over a million civilians left Vietnam when the communists took over in 1975
- Known as boat people, many of them eventually resettled in North American and European countries

FACT FILE

The cost to the USA's reputation at home and abroad

- The Vietnam War split opinion in America into supporters and opponents
- Although communism did not spread to Thailand or India as some US politicians feared, Vietnam became a communist state, as did Laos and Cambodia
- American actions during the Vietnam War – such as the My Lai massacre, the bombing of Cambodia, the Watergate scandal and the shooting of American student protesters – all damaged people's belief in the government and America's claim to lead the world in promoting freedom and peace

FACT FILE

Vietnam's reputation after the war

- Vietnam continued to face hostility from the USA after the war
- US President Ford opposed Vietnam joining the United Nations; this isolated Vietnam from the wider international community
- Vietnam emerged from the war as a united country, but many who lived in the south resented the communist rule imposed on them

SUMMARY

- US President Nixon used a range of strategies to end the USA's involvement in the war.
- Peace talks began in Paris in January 1969 – and the Paris Peace Accord was agreed and signed in January 1973.
- In December 1974, North Vietnam attacked South Vietnam. In April 1975, South Vietnam's capital fell to the communists and Vietnam was again a unified country, under communist control.
- There are many reasons to explain why the US approach in Vietnam failed, and why the approach of the Vietcong and North Vietnamese army was a success.
- The Vietnam War had a major and long-lasting impact on both the USA and Vietnam.

⚙ APPLY

HOW FAR DO YOU AGREE?

a   Create a series of flashcards that show the impact of the Vietnam War.

b   Do you think the war was a complete disaster for the USA? Explain your answer.

c   **EXAM QUESTION** 'The cost in human life was the main consequence of the war in Vietnam.' How far do you agree with this statement? Explain your answer.

EXAMINER TIP

Don't spend too long on an introduction to this type of question because you won't pick up many marks for it. However, it's important to make your overall opinion clear from the start of the essay to show that your judgement is sustained.

EXAMINER TIP

Look at the name given to each character and try to explain why the characters at the bar are dressed differently and are different sizes.

SOURCE ANALYSIS

▼ **SOURCE A** *A cartoon published in the* Washington Post, *26 January 1965. The man on the left is called 'Military establishments', the man on the right is called 'Arms costs' and the man in the middle is called 'Health, education and welfare'*

"Kindly Move Over A Little, Gentlemen"

EXAM QUESTION **Source A** is critical of the amount of money spent on the Vietnam War. How do you know? Explain your answer using **Source A** and your contextual knowledge.

Exam practice

GCSE sample answers

 REVIEW

On these exam practice pages, you will find a sample student answer for each of the exam questions for Paper 1: Section B: Conflict and Tension in Asia 1950–1975. What are the strengths and weaknesses of the answers? Read the following pages and think carefully about what the student has written, what the examiner has said about each answer, and how you might improve your own answers to the Conflict and Tension exam questions.

Source analysis questions

▶ **SOURCE A** *A cartoon published in an American newspaper, the* Washington Star, *in April 1965. It shows Ho Chi Minh as an octopus and the USA cutting its tentacles*

 1 Study **Source A**. **Source A** is supportive of US bombing raids in Vietnam. How do you know?

4 marks

Sample student answer

I know that the cartoon supports US bombing raids in Vietnam because it shows Ho Chi Minh as an octopus wrapping its tentacles around South Vietnam. The USA is seen cutting off the octopus' tentacles and freeing South Vietnam from Ho Chi Minh's grip. The scissors that are cutting the South off from Ho Chi Minh represent US air strikes. By freeing South Vietnam from the clutches of the evil creature, that represents the spread of communism, it is clear the cartoonist is in support of US bombing raids.

EXAMINER TIP

There is no contextual knowledge here. It would be good to include some information about the bombing raids and how they were used to stop Ho Chi Minh's forces.

OVERALL COMMENT

This response would achieve a Level 1. The student has used evidence from the Source to describe parts of the cartoon and explain what they represent. To develop the answer, so that it would achieve a level 2, the student should use their own knowledge to explain how the bombing raids would have helped South Vietnam in its battle with the North.

OVER TO YOU

1 Review the sample answer:

    a highlight anywhere that the student used evidence from the source

    b underline the sentences where the student directly answers the question about how they know the source is supportive of US bombing raids in Vietnam.

2 **a** Now have a go at writing your own answer. You should spend around five minutes on this type of question.

    b Review your answer. Did you…

        ☐ use specific evidence from the source?

        ☐ use your own knowledge and give at least one example of how the bombing raids were used to stop Ho Chi Minh's forces.

        ☐ make sure your answer is focused on the question by using the same wording in your answer?

Go back to Chapters 5–7 to refresh your knowledge of US tactics during the Vietnam War.

▼ **SOURCE B** *The cover of a comic book for students, published in 1960. America is a boat sailing towards an iceberg that represents communism. The tombstones are countries that are part of the USSR*

▼ **SOURCE C** *An extract from a press conference with President Eisenhower in 1954, where he explains his Domino Theory. The countries he mentions are all near Vietnam*

You have a row of dominoes set up, you knock over the first one, and what will happen to the last one is the certainty that it will go over very quickly, the loss of Indochina, of Burma, of Thailand, of the Peninsula, and Indonesia following. Now you begin to talk about areas that not only multiply the disadvantages that you would suffer through loss of sources of materials, but now you are talking about millions and millions and millions of people. The possible consqequences of the loss are just incalcuable to the free world.

 2 Study **Sources B** and **C**. How useful are **Sources B** and **C** to a historian studying US involvement in Vietnam? Explain your answer using **Sources B** and **C** and your contextual knowledge. `12 marks`

Sample student answer

In Source B we can see a boat symbolising America sailing towards an iceberg that could sink it. On the iceberg there are tombstones with the names of countries that have become communist. This suggests that the USA is worried about the spread of communism. There was a feeling in America that the communist threat from Europe, the Soviet Union and China could spread to America. This feeling was known as the Red Scare. It led to increased US involvement in Vietnam because China was supplying the Vietcong with money and equipment, making it harder for the South Vietnamese government to fight Ho Chi Minh and the Vietcong. This source is, therefore, useful because it shows a key reason for US involvement in Vietnam.

Source C is useful because it explains President Eisenhower's Domino Theory. It shows that America was worried about communism spreading, so they sent support to the ARVN.

EXAMINER TIP

Here, the student analyses the content of the source and supports it with accurate and relevant contextual knowledge.

EXAMINER TIP

The student makes a statement about Source C but does not explain the statement using information taken from the source or the source's provenance. To push for a Level 4 this paragraph needs to be developed.

OVERALL COMMENT

This response would achieve a top Level 2. To improve this answer, the student should comment on the provenance of the other source. For example, they should consider the usefulness of the source in relation to when and where it was created, and what you know about the author's beliefs, access to information and purpose.

OVER TO YOU

1   Now have a go at the question yourself. You should spend around 15 minutes on this type of question. Read the overall comment carefully and think about what you would need to add or change in order to achieve a Level 4.

2   Review your answer. Did you…

☐ read the question carefully and make sure you addressed everything it asks you to do? For example, did you use both sources in your answer and explain them both?

☐ identify what each source tells about US involvement in Vietnam and use details (a quote from a written source or a description of a visual source) as evidence to support your ideas?

☐ link each source to your own knowledge in order to explain how useful the sources are to a historian studying US involvement in Vietnam?

☐ use the information in the captions (provenance)?

Go back to Chapter 4–6 to help refresh your knowledge of the reasons for increased US involvement in Vietnam.

EXAMINER TIP

When analysing and evaluating a source, it's a good idea to look at the provenance. This will help you decide how useful the source is. If it is one-sided or unreliable it may not be useful to a historian for the purpose stated in the question.

The 'write an account' question

 Write an account of how the UN army attack at Inchon led to an international crisis. **8 marks**

Sample student answer

The UN army attack at Inchon led to an international crisis because UN forces had to fight North Korean forces to recapture Inchon and the South Korean capital city of Seoul. This led to the UN forces crossing the 38th parallel into North Korea.

Another reason that the events surrounding the attack at Inchon led to an international crisis was because it led to China joining North Korean forces. As the UN forces moved north, the Chinese issued a warning: UN forces should stop or China would join the war. McArthur was so certain that China would not join the war that he told Truman that UN forces should continue to advance. However, he was wrong. China sent 200,000 troops to join North Korea. They pushed the UN forces back and re-took Seoul. This created an international crisis because the UN forces were now engaged in war with both North Korea and China.

OVERALL COMMENT

This answer achieves a Level 3 because the student has explained their second point but not their first point. This response would gain a higher mark if the first point was explained and the how the first event led to the second event was also explained.

OVER TO YOU

1   Have a go at answering the question yourself. Try to think about the consequences for the Korean War but also the other countries involved. You should spend around 10 minutes on your answer.

2   Review your answer. Did you…

☐ explain at least two events concerning the UN attack at Inchon that led to an international crisis?

☐ make sure your answer is focused on the question by using the same wording in your answer?

☐ explain the consequences of the attack in relation to the USSR, China and the UN?

Go to pages 18–23 to help refresh your knowledge of the attack at Inchon.

The 'how far do you agree' question

 'The main reason for changing American public opinion towards the Vietnam War was its cost.' How far do you agree with this statement? Explain your answer. | 16 marks | SPaG 4 marks |

EXAMINER TIP

Don't forget that you can pick up marks here for showing the examiner that you can use spelling, punctuation and grammar correctly. It is worth factoring in some time to check your answer at the end. Make sure you write in paragraphs and that you use capital letters for proper nouns. Try to use historical terms; the glossary at the back of this book can help you become familiar with terms that could be useful in your exam.

Sample student answer

Although the cost of war was an important reason for changing American public opinion, I believe that American tactics used during the Vietnam War was the main reason public opinion towards the war changed.

Most Americans supported the war in its early days due to the fear of communism spreading across the globe. However, when reports of American tactics reached the US, through TV and newspaper reports, many people changed their opinion. This was most evident after Seymour Hersch uncovered the events at My Lai. Newspapers revealed that Charlie Company had killed innocent civilians, including many women and children, during a search and destroy mission to find the Vietcong. They then lied about the number of civilians who had died, claiming they had killed Vietcong fighters. Further reports of children being severely injured by Napalm and children being born with birth defects after their mothers were exposed to Agent Orange while pregnant, made many Americans question their support for the war. Without the media, many Americans would not have known about the impact of US tactics on innocent civilians. The media also helped to change public opinion during the Tet Offensive, when it became clear from TV reports that the Vietcong were not being defeated despite years of US involvement.

The role of the media not only changed public opinion because American citizens were made aware of the cost to civilian lives, it also became clear that the money being spent on the war was not worth it; the Tet Offensive was a spark for this. President Johnson had promised to invest money in his 'Great Society' scheme, to help those living in poverty, but had spent the money on the war instead. Those involved in the civil rights movement also changed their opinion of the war when it became clear that more black men were being sent to war than white men because black men could not 'dodge' the draft.

EXAMINER TIP

The student has used the wording from the question throughout the answer to show the response is focused on the question.

EXAMINER TIP

This point would benefit from more facts and figures regarding the casulties, deaths, and actual money spent on the war.

Furthermore, Martin Luther King thought that Johnson should have invested in the Great Society to help black people, while Muhammad Ali felt that the real war was at home and that the fight was for civil rights and not against the Vietcong.

EXAMINER TIP

This answer would have benefited from a clear final judgement about the main reason for public opinion towards the Vietnam War changing in America. The judgement should summarise the different reasons for the change in public opinion, evaluate the relative importance of each reason and decide which was most important in changing public opinion.

OVERALL COMMENT

This answer would achieve a top Level 3 because it has two explained points, although the second point would benefit from more evidence. To secure a Level 4, the student would need to give a clear judgement about the main reason for public opinion towards the Vietnam War changing in America.

OVER TO YOU

1   Explanation is the key to getting a good level in this type of question. Go through the answer and underline each time the student explains by linking their ideas back to the question.

2   Create a flashcard summarising the evidence and arguments that you could use if you were asked this question in the exam.

3   Use your flashcard to improve the answer above by adding more evidence to the second point and writing a judgement paragraph.

4   Review your answer. Did you…

☐   include both sides of the argument?

☐   mention specific evidence – events, dates etc. – to support your ideas?

☐   link back to the question at the end of each paragraph to help you to explain your ideas?

☐   use accurate spelling, punctuation and grammar?

☐   include a clear judgment that runs all the way through your answer?

Go back to Chapters 6 and 8 to help refresh your knowledge of changing public opinion in America towards the Vietnam War.

The answers provided here are examples, based on the information provided in the Recap sections of this Revision Guide. There may be other factors which are relevant to each question, and you should draw on as much of your own knowledge as possible to give detailed and precise answers. There are also many ways of answering exam questions (for example, of structuring an essay). However, these exemplar answers should provide a good starting point.

Chapter 1

Page 13

WRITE AN ACCOUNT

a **Cold War:** the time when relations between the USA (and allies) and the USSR (and allies) were openly hostile

containment: US policy aimed at stopping the spread of communism

NATO: military alliance of the USA, Britain, France and other countries formed as a defence against the USSR and allies

Warsaw Pact: military alliance Led by the USSR, and containing the USSR, Albania, Bulgaria, Czechoslovakia, East Germany, Hungary, Poland and Romania

b You should base your diagram on the communism and capitalism spider diagrams on page 12.

c Reasons might include: disagreement and suspicion over rival political systems; disagreement over what to do with the countries devastated by the Second World War; fear of communism in the west – and communist expansion; anger by USSR over the Truman Doctrine and containment; mutual fear over each other's military power (nuclear); division of nations into two rival pacts (NATO and Warsaw Pact) heightened tension further.

Page 15

SOURCE ANALYSIS

a In the early 1900s, Japan took over Korea; Korea remained under Japanese control until the end of the Second World War. After the war, Japanese soldiers in the north of Korea surrendered to Soviet forces and Japanese soldiers in

the south surrendered to US forces; the country was divided into two separate zones. This division was meant to be temporary; it was intended that Korea should become a united, independent country. Elections were planned, organised by the United Nations. Before elections were organised, Soviets in the northern zone allowed a Korean communist named Kim Il-sung to take power; no elections were held there. In the US-controlled southern zone, elections were held; a capitalist with strong ties to the USA (Syngman Rhee) became leader.

b Two political systems on one peninsula; communism right next to capitalism; both regimes heavily supported by USA and USSR; only a short time after the Truman Doctrine and the USA's commitment to containment; China 'fell' to communism, so the USA was worried about the spread of communism; US spies reported Stalin's determination to spread communism.

c **Syngman Rhee:** leader of capitalist South Korea

Kim Il-sung: leader of communist North Korea

President Truman: US President committed to containment

Chiang Kai-shek: leader of the Chinese government

Mao Tse-tung: Chinese communist leader

d Truman is referring to the capitalist system (like the USA) and the communist system (like the USSR).

e Truman describes one as democratic ('based upon the will of the majority'), and with freedoms (such as free elections, and freedom of speech and religion). He is referring to the system in the USA here because later he says it is the USA's job to ensure this happens. He describes the other system as one that is not democratic and one of 'terror and oppression', tight government control and limited freedoms.

f You could write that Source A is useful because it is the words of a US President – and the President is the one who often leads foreign policy and shapes opinions, and who often reflects the opinion of the electorate. It also

shows the historian the motives for the American policy against communism. You could write that Source B is useful because it reflects the concern in many countries (in this case, New Zealand) that communism will expand beyond China and into Malaya, Tibet, French Indochina and Korea. Both sources reflect a fear and concern that communism will engulf the world.

Page 17

HOW FAR DO YOU AGREE

a Your timeline might include:
  • **Early 1949:** North Korean leader, Kim Il-sung, visits Soviet leader Stalin to ask for support for an invasion. Stalin does not think the time is right (US soldiers are still based in South Korea and an invasion by the North might pull Soviet soldiers into a fight with US troops).
  • **Spring 1950:** Stalin believes the situation has changed – US troops have left Korea, there has been a communist revolution in nearby China, the Soviets have developed their own nuclear weapons and feel a more equal military opponent to the USA; they have also managed to crack secret US codes used to communicate with other governments around the world. The USSR begins to supply tanks, artillery and aircraft to North Korea, and begins to train soldiers.
  • **April 1950:** Stalin gives Kim Il-sung permission to invade South Korea – he makes it clear that Soviet troops will not be directly involved. He says that if reinforcements are needed, they must come from China, not from the USSR.
  • **25 June 1950:** North Korean troops invade South Korea.
  • **27 June 1950:** President Truman declares that the USA will go to the aid of South Korea. He also says that the UN Security Council must meet quickly to decide how to respond.

b **Kim Il-sung:** leader of country that invaded, so his decision. Actively sought approval to invade from the USSR

Stalin: gave support for invasion, although stated that Russian troops would not be directly involved.

Suggested China as an alternative source of troops

Communist China: was to be a source of troops/support; openly supported North Korea

President Truman: the Truman Doctrine was an aggressive stance against communism

The UN: allowed US to dominate, and their stance was anti-communist

Syngman Rhee: relied on US support; failure to build up forces made South Korea an easier target

c **The UN:** orders North to leave South, assembles a UN force

The USA: sends US fleet to area, under MacArthur

The USSR: condemns UN response and criticises USA

d Your answer should reflect the North Korean leader's role in the outbreak of war, but also pick up on the role played by other factors, such as the USA's aggressive stance towards communism and Stalin's approval of the actions of North Korea and his encouragement of the aggression.

Chapter 2

Page 19

WRITE AN ACCOUNT

a Your answers will vary but an example for 'The United Nations at War' could include:

- North Korean forces quickly pushed South Korean army back towards Pusan
- 15 September 1950: UN troops launched surprise attack from sea at Inchon
- Inchon was quickly captured; then UN pushed inland to recapture Seoul
- UN forces and South Korean troops in the south advanced north
- By early October, all North Korean troops had been driven out of South Korea, back behind the 38th parallel

b This might be due to the US desire to contain communism, and the US dominance of the UN strategy. The UN hoped it might unite Korea. Truman wanted to be tough on communism.

c Your answer will focus on the fact that the war (which began as a conflict between North and South Korea) developed into a conflict involving some of the most powerful nations in the world: North Korean forces pushed back the South Korean army; UN troops from 16 nations attacked at Inchon, then pushed inland to recapture Seoul; also UN and South Korean troops in the south advanced north; North Korean troops were driven behind the 38th parallel; China's leader (Mao Tse-tung) warned UN not to advance towards China; when UN troops got near the Yalu River on the Chinese border, around 200,000 Chinese troops joined the North Koreans to fight back; the USSR supplied China; UN forces pushed back.

SOURCE ANALYSIS

a He was the US-born Commander-in-Chief of the UN forces.

b Despite being ordered not to by President Truman, MacArthur sent UN troops back into North Korea. He said he wanted to unite Korea and demanded a Chinese surrender. He said that the USA should be prepared to use nuclear weapons if necessary. Truman was furious with MacArthur's refusal to follow orders and sacked him.

c You could write that the source shows MacArthur, in military uniform, moving the USA (shown by the hat) towards another world war (WWIII). The cartoon shows that MacArthur's actions are responsible for moving the USA nearer to war – and they are already in a precarious situation, shown by the fact that they are on the edge of a cliff. He is shown as negative/aggressive, and the cartoon suggests dire consequences flowing from his actions.

Chapter 3

Page 21

SOURCE ANALYSIS

a **stalemate:** a situation in which neither side can make progress

defect: leave a country or side to join an opposing one

demilitarised zone: area from which weapons and soldiers have been removed

b They used their vast airpower to bomb North Korean towns, cities, transport systems, factories and military bases with high explosives and napalm; tried to steal Soviet air technology to gain the upper hand; arranged peace talks.

c You should produce your own fact test for this activity.

d You could write that this source shows the Korean War was a proxy war – a war fought by countries other than Korea. The source shows how involved both China and the USSR were in the Korean War. Source B shows a US military tactic: the MiG-15 Soviet fighter jets were so much better than any of the UN fighter planes that the Americans offered a large reward to any Chinese, North Korean or Soviet pilot who was prepared to defect, to fly to a UN airfield and hand his technologically-advanced plane over to the Americans, who could then copy the Soviet technology.

Page 23

HOW FAR DO YOU AGREE

a Your answer might include:

- It meant the Cold War had spread from Europe to Asia
- USA made additional alliances with countries in the east, such as the Philippines, Australia and New Zealand
- USA spent vast sums of money rebuilding Japan
- USA cut off all dealings with communist China; instead gave its support to the politicians who had controlled China before the communist takeover (now based on the island of Taiwan)
- USA vowed to increase support (such as supplies and weapons) for any country fighting communism, such as the French who were fighting communist rebels in French-controlled Vietnam
- Both the US and Soviet armies, navies and air forces increased in size at this time too – the US army, for example, increased by 50%
- USA increased the number of army and air bases outside US territory in Europe, the Middle East, and elsewhere in Asia

- Increase in quality and quantity of nuclear weapons on both sides; increased spending on military by both sides

b You will create your own chart for this activity.

c Your answer should focus on the fact that there were some gains and losses on both sides, with some gaining more than others, but there were no clear winners. You may emphasise that it was a political victory in one sense for the USA, as they managed to contain communism, but it cost them a relationship with China and heightened Cold War tension in the region. You might also mention that Korea itself was the clear loser.

SOURCE ANALYSIS

Source A is an anti-USSR poster, dropped by US-led UN forces, showing the negative side of Soviet involvement in Korea. The USSR is shown as aggressive (the snake is squeezing/hurting Korean people and soldiers – representing civilian and military casualties). The skull indicates death/destruction due to Soviet involvement in Korea. The poster was dropped as propaganda so it is deliberately hostile to the USSR.

Chapter 4

Page 25

WRITE AN ACCOUNT

a Your cards could include: French control; American financial aid to help the French; creation of Vietminh; First Indochina War; Battle of Dien Bien Phu; Vietminh guerrilla tactics; American support for Diem; Geneva Agreement.

b The events above are shown in chronological order. You may find that some cards have multiple lines between them. Your links should be focused on how each event increased tension in Vietnam.

c You should write about US support for South Vietnam and the Diem regime and how this was an international issue because it forced the North, under Ho Chi Minh, to seek support from other powers. You could also mention the Geneva Agreement of 1954, which split

Vietnam in two and called for elections. This became an international issue when Diem called an early election. This annoyed people, who decided to support the Vietcong as a result.

Page 27

WRITE AN ACCOUNT

a Your mind-map may include the following: Diem pushed peasants off their land; he gave top jobs to his family and friends; he punished (sometimes by death) any opposition; he called an election in South Vietnam in October 1955 and rigged this election; he put restrictions on Buddhists and how they could worship.

b Your answers may include:

NLF: they didn't like the way Diem had pushed peasants off their land; they wanted a united Vietnam; eventually, they became a communist group and they wanted a communist government

Buddhists: they wanted to worship without having to ask for permission

c Diem called an early election so he could take control of South Vietnam and get rid of Bo Dai. He knew if he waited until 1956 there was a chance that Ho Chi Minh would win.

d The Americans were scared about the spread of communism and were certain that Ho Chi Minh would win the election in 1956. If the election was held in 1955 then Diem would win and America would have someone in control in Vietnam that they could influence.

e One reason tension increased in South Vietnam was because of Diem calling an early election. This was his way of securing power in South Vietnam but he also used intimidation to get people to vote for him. During the election, the US government supported Diem. Many people turned to the Vietcong because they were so frustrated with Diem's way of running the country. This caused tension as opposition to Diem grew.

Opposition to Diem was strong amongst Buddhists who felt that Diem's new religious policies were anti-Buddhist – one being that Buddhists had to have permission to worship. This

caused tension as Buddhists publically opposed Diem gaining a lot of media coverage.

Page 29

HOW FAR DO YOU AGREE

a Your answer might include: to unite Vietnam; to remove the American presence in Vietnam; land reform.

b America helped the AVRN by sending money and supplies and training ARVN soldiers.

c The military tactics of the Vietcong were guerrilla tactics that worked by targeting poorly defended ARVN bases. They worked in small groups and could not be identified as they did not wear a uniform.

d Diem calling an early election in 1955 led to civil war in South Vietnam because it meant that Diem had broken the 1954 Geneva Agreement and had angered Ho Chi Minh and the North. Diem rigged the election and, with American support, tricked people into voting for him. This was a longer-term cause of the civil war. Other factors could include: American involvement (the people of Vietnam had been treated badly by the French and would not appreciate another foreign power in the region; furthermore, it was clear that the USA did not want communism in South Vietnam); the creation of the NLF (this organised the opposition to Diem and provided a group to fight Diem during the civil war).

Chapter 5

Page 31

SOURCE ANALYSIS

a **Cold War:** tension after the Second World War between the USA and USSR; a fight between communism and capitalism

Marshall Plan: the USA's financial scheme to give countries money to rebuild and stop them becoming communist

Domino Theory: if one country falls to communism then neighbouring countries will fall too

b The Red Scare was the paranoia about communism that spread across

America after the Second World War. Many people were worried that there were Soviet spies in America. This led to McCarthyism.

c Source A is useful to a historian studying American fears about the spread of communism as the source states that the communist government of North Vietnam was trying to take over a neighbouring state. This refers to the civil war in South Vietnam, where NLF cells were fighting the ARVN after Diem called an early election. Source A is useful because the State Department published the statement, which means it represents the official American government view and shows that the American government believed in the Domino Theory (if one country fell to communism then other countries nearby would too). The State Department particularly feared communism spreading to South Vietnam because this would mean it would spread to Laos and Cambodia as well. The source is also useful for telling us about American fears about the spread of communism as the words 'conquer' and 'rebellion' give us the impression that Ho Chi Minh and the NLF are in the wrong; this is clearly American propaganda, making it useful to a historian.

Source B is also useful because it shows an octopus, which represents the Soviet Union, a communist country, spreading communism all over the world. The octopus is big and red and has Stalin's face. Stalin looks angry. We can learn from this that Americans feared communism because they saw it as aggressive. The source illustrates the Domino Theory. The source is clearly American propaganda and was created at a time when many Americans feared the 'Red Scare', which increased with McCarthyism.

Page 33
SOURCE ANALYSIS

a Eisenhower helped Diem by sending US soldiers to train ARVN soldiers; he also helped Diem win the 1955 election.

b The Strategic Hamlet Programme was a way for the USA to cut off the support the peasants were giving the Vietcong,

by moving them away from their villages and into 'hamlets' surrounded by barbed wire and ditches.

c The coup against Diem was when his generals and soldiers in the ARVN rebelled against him and shot him dead on 2 November 1963.

d You could describe what you can see in the source: an American soldier struggling to walk up the stairs as there are children's toys under his feet making him fall; the soldier represents the help America sent and the toys show the problems in South Vietnam. You could then put this into context: by 1964 America was sending more military equipment and men were having to engage in battle to defend themselves. The Strategic Hamlet Programme had been a failure and had resulted in more support for Ho Chi Minh. Diem was an unpopular leader and would not be influenced by America. Kennedy had only wanted to train ARVN fighters but by the time of his assassination he was spending more money and sending more military advisers and equipment.

Chapter 6
Page 35
SOURCE ANALYSIS

a Johnson believed in Eisenhower's Domino Theory so felt it was important for the USA to keep supporting South Vietnam. However he was reluctant to send US troops to fight in Vietnam because he knew this would make him unpopular with voters in the USA.

b Johnson tried to combat communism in Vietnam by approving Operation 3A, which increased the US presence in Vietnam. He sent South Vietnamese mercenaries to the North and he sent US destroyers to the waters of North Vietnam.

c It was important for US involvement in Vietnam because it led to the Gulf of Tonkin Resolution, which increased US military powers in Vietnam. It also led to Operation Rolling Thunder.

d This was the continuous dropping of bombs in North Vietnam. It was designed to destroy morale and weaken Ho Chi Minh's support for the

Vietcong.

e The source is critical of Johnson because it shows him dropping bombs, which are the leaves on his olive branch, onto a Vietnamese village; the artist has drawn a black sky to show that there is either a lot of smoke or that Johnson is bringing a storm with him; the fact that he is dropping bombs on a village is critical of Johnson because it shows the USA is killing civilians; this cartoon was drawn a year after the introduction of Operation Rolling Thunder which was a bombing campaign on North Vietnam – it marked a change in US involvement in the war; on the dove (Johnson) it says 'LBJ Vietnam Peace Drive' – this is critical of Johnson because he said he was committed to not sending combat troops to Vietnam so he could be re-elected. Once elected he sent troops to fight in Vietnam

Page 37
WRITE AN ACCOUNT

a The Ho Chi Minh-trail that went from North Vietnam, through Laos and Cambodia, to South Vietnam. It was used to take supplies to the Vietcong.

b 'Hanging on the belts' was the tactic of the Vietcong of staying close to the US soldiers and ambushing them. Because the Vietcong did not wear a uniform it made it easy for them to attack the US soldiers and then disappear in to the jungle without being identified.

c The Vietcong had the following advantages: the Ho Chi Minh trail; they did not have a uniform; they used underground tunnels; they set booby traps; they had the support of the villagers; they knew the jungle.

d The American troops would have been nervous, anxious and scared as the Vietcong were constantly taking them by surprise with their guerrilla tactics. The Vietcong 'hung on the belts' of the US troops and used booby traps. This meant the American troops would have been always on edge waiting for an attack.

e The Vietcong fought a psychological war because they always took the US troops by surprise. They would 'hang on their belts' and use booby traps to keep the US troops in constant fear that they would be attacked. This had a psychological impact because the US troops could not plan for these attacks. They never knew when Vietcong fighters were planning an attack because the Vietcong did not wear a uniform; this meant American troops never knew where their enemy was. The Vietcong also used their tunnel systems and the Ho Chi Minh trail to fight a psychological war because they could easily hide their supplies and fighters and the US troops could not find them.

Page 39
HOW FAR DO YOU AGREE

a   Your answer might include: guns jammed in wet and dirty conditions; difficulties telling the difference between Vietcong and civilians; most were young and inexperienced.

b   **search and destroy:** looking in villages for Vietcong fighters. If suspects were found the village would be destroyed in raids known as 'zippo' raids

   Agent Orange: chemical weedkiller used to clear the jungle. Caused deformities in unborn babies, and cancer

   napalm: highly flammable liquid that would burn through the thick jungle but also burnt through skin and bones

   Operation Rolling Thunder: continuous bombing campaign on North Vietnam

c   Many villagers turned against the US forces because their tactics targeted innocent civilians. It was hard for the Americans to identify the Vietcong, which meant they often targeted peasants. This can be seen in their search and destroy tactics. Furthermore, their use of chemical warfare made the people of Vietnam more sympathetic to the Vietcong. Many children were born with deformities because of Agent Orange, and napalm injured many.

d   American tactics were one of the reasons the Vietnam War went on for so long. Their search and destroy tactics, operation rolling thunder and the use of chemical warfare pushed

the Vietnamese people into supporting the Vietcong. This meant US troops faced more opposition than they might otherwise have done, and so the war went on longer. However, American tactics were not the only reason the Vietnam War went on for so long. The Vietcong knew the jungle well and were able to outsmart US combat troops, using booby traps and surprise attacks, which meant the US could never get an advantage and end the war. It also went on for so long because the Americans were fighting a long-distance war. Vietnam is over 12,000 kilometres from the USA and there were often supply issues with equipment and weaponry.

Page 41
WRITE AN ACCOUNT

a   The Vietcong – Charlie Company thought My Lai was a Vietcong base.

b   They lied about the numbers of Vietcong and civilians killed, e.g. Colonel Barker reported that 128 Vietcong soldiers had been killed but in fact three Vietcong were killed at the start of the operation by gunships and none were found by Charlie Company. They covered up the killing of innocent civilians.

c   It would undermine American confidence in the US army because it exposed the low morale of the US troops in Vietnam. It also showed the cruel treatment of civilians at the hands of US soldiers.

d   You could list the following key words: children, women, murder, Calley, Charlie Company, anti-war movement, morale, investigation, public opinion, media. You should use your five chosen words and link them to the events during and after My Lai.

e   Your account could include: the events of My Lai showed the American public how difficult it was for US forces to stop the Vietcong; My Lai made many people wonder why civilians were being targeted when US involvement was meant to be about containing communism; it showed the inexperience of the soldiers who were fighting in Vietnam and how low morale was among the troops; people began to mistrust the army when it was clear there had been a cover up; the images in the media of women and

children being killed gave rise to the anti-war movement.

Page 43
HOW FAR DO YOU AGREE

a   The Tet Offensive was when the Vietcong broke a ceasefire in January 1968 and attacked towns, cities and US bases and buildings. It was an attempt to get the people of South Vietnam to rise up against the government and US forces. The Vietcong were eventually defeated.

b   It increased opposition to the war because it showed how, despite the billions of dollars being spent on the war, the Vietcong were not weakened. Furthermore, 300 US troops were being killed every week – the US public started to doubt if the financial and human cost of the war was worth it.

c   Your mind map should include: US tactics; the treatment of civilians; My Lai; Tet Offensive; cost of war – both economic and human; anti-war movement.

d   You should annotate your mind-map; your annotations will depend on the reasons you have included.

e   You should select what you believe to have been the main cause of increased opposition.

f   Your answer might suggest that the Tet Offensive was the main reason for the increased opposition to the Vietnam War as it highlighted all the problems in the war in one event. It was shown on TV, therefore the American people could see how strong the Vietcong were. The American people had supported the war in the early days, however, by 1968, opinion polls showed that the public doubted the cost of war was worth it – 300 soldiers a week were being killed and the billions of dollars being spent were not securing an American victory. This was money that Johnson had originally said was for the Great Society. The Tet Offensive also shows the importance of the media in increasing opposition because images appeared on TV of civilians being killed. This was also the case with My Lai. The Civil Rights Movement was another contributing factor to increased opposition as disproportionately more black men were sent to fight. Many black people felt that they had a more important fight at home to improve their civil rights.

Chapter 7

Page 45

SOURCE ANALYSIS

a **Vietnamisation:** the policy Richard Nixon introduced to take US troops out of Vietnam.

b Bombing Cambodia and Laos would help because it would destroy Vietcong bases and would stop the Vietcong getting supplies down the Ho Chi Minh Trail.

c Vietnamisation achieved the following: by the end of 1969 85,000 troops had returned home to the USA; it paved the way for Nixon to work with China and the USSR to end the fighting in Vietnam.

d Nixon's policy of Vietnamisation failed in the following ways: in 1970 he sent another 150,000 US soldiers into Vietnam to help with the bombing of Cambodia; US troops entered Laos in 1971 and the attack was a failure; in 1972 a napalm bomb was dropped in South Vietnam, killing and injuring innocent civilians.

e Nixon is riding two horses: one named 'no surrender', the other 'Vietnamisation'. The 'no surrender' horse is running away from Nixon and the 'Vietnamisation' horse is on its knees. Nixon is sweating and finding it hard to control both horses.

f **I can tell that the source criticises Nixon's policy of Vietnamisation because ...** the horse named 'Vietnamisation' is on its knees.

This suggests that ... the policy of Vietnamisation was failing.

Vietnamisation was seen as a failure because ... it took so long to withdraw US troops that Nixon approved a bombing attack of Cambodia to target Vietcong bases. This resulted in many civilians being killed.

Chapter 8

Page 47

WRITE AN ACCOUNT

a You should create your own mnemonic or acronym for this activity, such as: **m**y **c**ar **d**oesn't **c**arry **l**arge **p**eople **w**ell;

or **m**y **c**at **d**oes **c**artwheels **s**ometimes, **p**retty **w**eird; to remind you about **m**edia coverage, **c**asualties, '**d**raft', **C**ivil Rights Movement, **l**ack of support/**s**upport, **p**oliticians, **w**inning.

b Your list could include: protest was particularly strong among college and university students; to many students the war symbolised the control and authority of government – they wanted to rebel against this; 'hippie culture' was popular with its key themes of peace and love; many anti-war demonstrations took place in 1968 and 1969; the largest anti-war protest in US history (500,000 people) took place in Washington on 15 November 1969; sometimes the protests ended in violence, when police and students clashed; the most infamous student demonstration occurred at Kent State University in Ohio in May 1970.

c Your answer should explain why opposition to the war increased (due to, for example, casualties, the draft system, media coverage, revelations about the My Lai massacre, bombing compaigns in Laos and Cambodia) and that opposition to the war was particularly strong among college and university students (because the war symbolised the control and authority of government – and students wanted to rebel against this). You should write about the shootings at Kent State University and how this both shocked the nation and led to an increase in opposition to the war, as many colleges and universities closed when two million students refused to attend classes. You could add that a similar incident occurred at Jackson State College (an all-black college in Mississippi), when police opened fire during a demonstration, killing two students and injuring twelve.

Page 49

SOURCE ANALYSIS

a When there were relatively few US troops in Vietnam, there was little coverage in newspapers, magazines and radio shows, or on television. Media coverage was generally positive – it focused on the bravery of the troops and their skill in handling

their new weapons. US troops were portrayed as the 'good guys' who were fighting the communist 'bad guys'.

b Video cameras and voice recorders were smaller and lighter, so recording news reports was a lot easier. Reporters were flown around the war zone by helicopter. The horrors of the war were captured in full colour, and pictures were sent back to the USA at great speed.

c Every day, the US army met with journalists in Vietnam. These 'press briefings' formed the basis of the journalists' news stories. Journalists joked that the army officials were not telling the true story of the war and were covering up how badly things were going at times.

d Source A tells us that increased media coverage allowed criticism of the war by very influential people to get into people's homes (Cronkite was 'the most trusted man in America'). It says that 'we are bogged down in stalemate'. Source B shows a soldier, who represents Uncle Sam/the US army, barely keeping his head above the quicksand. It represents a popular view at the time, created by news reports about the fighting and casualty figures, that the USA had become stuck in a conflict in Vietnam/Asia that it could not hope to win. Together, Sources A and B show that the American media, in its different forms, believed that the USA could not win the war in Vietnam.

Page 51

WRITE AN ACCOUNT

a You will create your own flashcards for this activity. For example:

Tet Offensive: began 30 January 1968; was a turning point in the way the war was reported, and how the US public viewed the war; it was widely reported by TV crews; it shocked the US public, who had no idea how brutal the fighting was; it made people question how much they could trust their government; it showed that the Vietcong were strong.

b This was when President Nixon (a Republican) was linked to a burglary at the offices of Nixon's rival party, the Democrats. His role in the cover-up led to his resignation.

c It came at a time when many Americans were already unhappy with the government over its role in cover-ups relating to the Vietnam War – My Lai and *New York Times* revelations, for example.

d You should write about the development of media and TV coverage (including, for example, the increase in reporters in Vietnam and increased TV ownership). You should then say how new technology – lightweight cameras, voice recorders – meant the horrors of the war could be captured in full colour and sent back to the USA at great speed. This meant that events like the Tet Offensive could be reported fully and the My Lai massacre investigated fully. These events turned opinion against the war and led to many mistrusting the government.

Chapter 9

Page 53
SOURCE ANALYSIS

a **Vietnamisation: Explanation** – Nixon's policy to build up the South Vietnamese army (ARVN) so it could carry on the war against the Vietcong and North Vietnamese without the help of US troops; **Reason** – US soldiers could return home because the South Vietnamese were strong enough to resist the North Vietnamese.

Pressure: Explanation – Nixon pressured South Vietnam's leaders to work out a deal with the North. He asked China and the USSR to pressurise North Vietnam into making deal; **Reason** – to end the war peacefully instead of continuing, with the waste of life and money.

Negotiation: Explanation – Nixon asked Kissinger to negotiate with North Vietnam; **Reason** – to bring about a ceasefire.

Bombing: Explanation – Nixon increased the bombing of North Vietnam and supply routes in Laos and Cambodia; **Reason** – to stop supplies reaching the Vietcong; he hoped to force the communists to look for peace.

b Your timeline will be based on the one on these pages, but should include 7 or 8 key events, such as: the US bombing raids on the Ho Chi Minh Trail in Cambodia; the first 25,000 US troops being withdrawn; the beginning of secret talks.

c You should write that the source is critical of Nixon's strategy to end the war in that he made a pledge to end the war in 1968, but the war is still continuing in 1972 (with 20,000 more dead Americans). The cartoonist is mocking Nixon's 1968 plans, which have not led to an end to the war.

Page 55
HOW FAR DO YOU AGREE

a You should create your own mind-map for this activity. For example, if you were writing about the impact of the media coverage as a factor, you might draw a TV screen and include the words 'TV coverage horrified the US public and the anti-war movement grew'.

b Reasons relating to the USA might include:

- Despite having the very latest high-tech military technology, the USA often killed innocent civilians or even their own troops. This had a demoralising effect on the soldiers, and had a major impact on the anti-war movement back in the USA.
- Many Americans questioned why the USA was fighting to defend the government of South Vietnam. They viewed it as brutal and corrupt.
- The discipline and morale of US troops was poor. Drug taking and desertion were common.
- A US soldier's 'tour of duty' was only one year long. After this time, he returned home. This meant soldiers never gained the necessary experience to fight in such tough conditions. Around 900 soldiers died on their first day in Vietnam.
- The Americans were fighting a long-distance war. Vietnam is over 12,000 kilometres from the USA and there were often supply issues with equipment and weaponry.
- The media coverage horrified the US public. As the war went on, it became more and more unpopular.

The anti-war movement was large and by the end of 1971 most Americans wanted the war to end as quickly as possible.

Reasons relating to the Vietcong and North Vietnamese army might include:

- The guerrilla tactics of the Vietcong were well suited to jungle warfare.
- Many South Vietnamese peasants supported the Vietcong. The peasants often helped the Vietcong.
- The Vietcong saw themselves as defending their own country against an American invasion. As a result, they fought with brutal determination to defend their homeland. The Vietcong were motivated by the thought of driving the USA out of Vietnam and uniting their country.
- The Vietcong were far more experienced than many of the soldiers they were fighting. They knew their territory well and had been fighting long before US troops arrived in Vietnam. They had fought the Japanese during the Second World War.
- The Vietcong were fighting on 'home soil' and were supplied locally or with equipment from allies in nearby China and the USSR.

c You should write about the impact of the TV and media coverage of the war, explaining how it helped to fuel a large anti-war movement, but you should also write about the impact of the other factors relating to the defeat, such as the guerrilla tactics of the Vietcong, the Vietcong's motivation to succeed, and the limitations of the US strategy.

SOURCE ANALYSIS

Source A is useful because it demonstrates the impact that the media, and television in particular, had on the war. Robin Day, a British news reporter, is not American and therefore possibly more objective about the USA and the Vietnam war. He claims that colour television was influential in forming American opinion about the Vietnam War, and goes so far as to say that the war was lost on American television screens. Source B is useful because it demonstrates the confusion in the minds of the American public about why the Americans are fighting in Vietnam, and the terrible mess that they got themselves into. The cartoon is critical and funny because it suggests that the soldiers in Vietnam have to find out from American newspapers why they are fighting, and the soldiers seem confused that nobody in America knows why they are fighting in Indochina.

Page 57

HOW FAR DO YOU AGREE

a You should create your own flashcards for this activity. For example, you could use the following categories: the financial cost of the war; the impact of the financial cost; the human cost of the war – USA; the human cost of the war – Vietnam; the environmental cost to Vietnam; the cost to the USA's reputation at home and abroad; Vietnam's reputation after the war.

b Your opinion will be based on the information you have read in this chapter, and might be informed by what you have learned in this particular spread. As with any answer of this type, you should back up your opinions with facts and figures. Also, where possible, try to balance your argument. For example, you might be leaning towards thinking that the war was a complete disaster but try to identify an area where it might not have been so disastrous.

c You should write about the cost of the war in terms of human life (for both Vietnam and the USA), explaining that the impact was not just death and injury, but also psychological. There are also the long-term health issues and birth defects associated with the chemicals used by the USA to consider. You must also remember to discuss the impact of other factors relating to the consequences of the war environmental damage; financial cost that impacted on domestic reforms in the USA; cost to both the USA's reputation at home and abroad and Vietnam's reputation after the war.

SOURCE ANALYSIS

The cartoon shows President Johnson as a bartender, representing the 'L. B. J. Budget'. The budget is the whole amount the President has to spend on foreign and domestic policies. He is asking two cowboys ('Military establishments' and 'Arms costs') to step aside and make some room at the bar for a small, impoverished fellow, 'Health, education and welfare'. By showing the two cowboys as large, well-armed and crowding out the smaller figure, the cartoonist is criticising the amount of money spent on the Vietnam War at the expense of domestic concerns such as health, education and welfare.

capitalist describing a political system that promotes the private ownership of factories and businesses in order to make a profit

communist describing a political ideology which promotes the common ownership of industry and production with no private owners

containment US policy of attempting to stop the spread of communism

Democrat a member of one of the two main political parties in US politics; often seen as more liberal

Domino Theory the idea that if one nation in a region fell under communist control, others would follow like toppling dominoes

Great Society President Lyndon Johnson's programme of reforms that aimed to make America a better, fairer society

Khmer Rouge communist organisation in Cambodia that became more popular in the early 1970s

mercenary a soldier who is paid by a foreign country to fight in its army

nationalist a person who supports political independence for a country

Republican a member of one of the two main political parties in US politics; often seen as more conservative

United Nations an international organisation formed in 1945 with headquarters in New York City, intended to promote international peace, security and cooperation

veto the right to block a decision made by others

Vietcong the communist guerrilla movement in Vietnam which fought South Vietnamese government forces between 1954 and 1975 with the support of the North Vietnamese army

Vietminh a communist-led organisation that fought against the Japanese and especially against the French in Indochina; many members of the Vietminh later joined with the Vietcong